leading
LIGHTS

First published in 2010 by
Liberties Press
Guinness Enterprise Centre | Taylor's Lane | Dublin 8
Tel: +353 (1) 415 1224

www.libertiespress.com | info@libertiespress.com
Distributed in the United States by
Dufour Editions | PO Box 7 | Chester Springs | Pennsylvania | 19425

and in Australia by
James Bennett Pty Limited | InBooks | 3 Narabang Way
Belrose NSW 2085

Trade enquiries to Gill & Macmillan Distribution
Hume Avenue | Park West | Dublin 12
Tel: +353 (1) 500 9534 | Fax: +353 (1) 500 9595
sales@gillmacmillan.ie

Copyright © Eamon Gilmore, 2010

The author has asserted his moral rights.

Paperback ISBN: 978-1-905483-39-6
Hardback ISBN: 978-1-907593-11-6
2 4 6 8 10 9 7 5 3 1
A CIP record for this title is available from the British Library.

Cover design by Sin É Design
Internal design by Liberties Press
Printed in Ireland by Colour Books

leading
LIGHTS

Eamon Gilmore
with Yseult Thornley

Dedicated to my late mother Celia, to my wife Carol, and to our children, Gráinne, Oisín and Seán

Contents

Introduction:
Why This Book?

At about 6.45 AM on the morning of 30 September 2008, I got one of the most dramatic and memorable telephone calls of my life. When I answered the phone, the person on the other end of the line was the Minister for Finance, Brian Lenihan. He was calling to inform me, as a courtesy, that the government would shortly be announcing a blanket guarantee of the liabilities of six Irish-owned banks.

After we talked for a while about the government's decision, I asked him if he would agree to me being briefed in more detail by the Department of Finance. He said he would arrange it. After I hung up, there was just time for a quick phone conversation with our finance spokesperson, Joan Burton, before *Morning Ireland* came on the radio, and the news of this fateful decision was broadcast to the nation.

As I drove into Leinster House to meet Joan and other colleagues, a strange mood was developing over the airwaves. As well as shock, there was a sort of euphoria among some commentators. For months, economic indicators for Ireland had been deeply worrying, and unemployment was increasing. Business people had been telling me that credit from the banks was drying up, but although I and others were raising this issue in the Dáil, the government seemed to be in denial about what was happening. Now, at least, there was something that looked like decisive action.

But was it the right decision? I had grave doubts, to put it mildly, but was determined not to pass judgement without hearing the arguments. I made a brief comment to the media in Leinster House, and then Joan and I went to be briefed by the Department of Finance on the background to the decision, and the detail of it. As we left that meeting, it was becoming clear to me that this was, at best, a bad decision, and at worst a potentially disastrous one.

As we walked back to Leinster House, government spin doctors were going into overdrive. It became clear that Labour would come under severe pressure to support the government's move, in the national interest, as Fine Gael were already doing. During that day, I met with several colleagues to discuss the approach we would take when the blanket guarantee was put to a vote in the Dáil. One of the biggest problems we faced was that there was so little hard information about the guarantee. What was the government asking the state – the taxpayer – to get into? What was the extent of our exposure? The government, including the Taoiseach, insisted that this was, in effect, a costless exercise. I remember thinking that if a favourite relative asked me to be his guarantor for a bank loan, I would at least want to know what kind of debts he had accumulated.

It quickly became evident that the blanket nature and extent of the guarantee were the problem. I knew that if we voted against the guarantee, it would be hard to explain our reasoning. In the previous weeks, there had been rumours about Anglo Irish Bank and Irish Nationwide Building Society, but to have repeated them in the Dáil would have been irresponsible, as it would probably have fuelled the growing lack of confidence in these institutions. Yet, at the same time, it was clear that Fianna Fáil was effectively writing a blank cheque to the banks and, incredibly, was taking no action to remove the failed management of these companies, especially in Anglo and Nationwide. It still amazes me that, for the next three months, Sean Fitzpatrick remained in charge of Anglo.

Of course, it would have been easy to join the consensus, as both Fine Gael and Sinn Féin were doing, and to support the guarantee, but we took the decision to oppose it. Not for the first or last time, this made us unpopular around Leinster House: Fianna Fáil began to proclaim loudly that Labour would prefer to let the banking system fail. Of course, we knew that they would do this, and I had no idea what that would do to Labour's standing in the country, but our judgement was that the government's decision was disastrously wrong, and we had to oppose it.

It gives me no pleasure to say that time has proven us to be correct. Three main factors – the failure of regulation, the greed of top bankers, speculation by property developers – each played a role in creating the property bubble that collapsed so dramatically and with such terrible consequences for the Irish people. And Fianna Fáil was strongly associated with all three of these things. Worst of all, the decision to give a blanket guarantee to the banks tied the Irish government – and the Irish people – to the banks at the hip. Thereafter, the bankers had the whip-hand, and government was floundering.

As I write this, the mess that Fianna Fáil has made of the crisis has destroyed Ireland's reputation abroad and brought the country to the edge of economic ruin. Back in September 2008, we didn't know what lay in the future; we simply had to make a judgement on the information at hand.

Now, as then, I believe that we made the right judgement for the right reasons. Ultimately, that is what this book is about. At the time of the bank guarantee, I had been leader of the Labour Party for about a year. I was starting to settle into the job, and indeed to enjoy it. The first three or four months had been hectic, as I built up my staff, thanked well-wishers, got used to the business of leading the party in the Dáil and prepared for the party conference in November – at which I would make my first major speech as leader. I was starting the work of modernising our party structures, building up our organisation, and encouraging Labour Party people to become more ambitious about the party's future.

By September 2008, we felt we were making progress. There were signs of a lift for Labour in the polls, and we were making headway with our internal-reform process. After the banking crisis broke, however, the pace of events accelerated rapidly. The mood in the country became steadily worse, and unemployment increased rapidly. In February 2009, when Brian Cowen announced to the

Dáil that the live register had reached 327,900 people, he was met, at first, with a stunned silence. Politics was also changing. Despite all the Fianna Fáil spin, it seemed that people were responding to Labour's stance on the banking crisis, and to our insistence that the jobs crisis could not be ignored. The level of interest in politics increased dramatically, as people saw the impact of the government's mistakes and failures on their own lives.

We continued to reform our party structures, to make Labour a more modern and efficient organisation and a more effective political force. This included a major change in our relationship with the trade union movement. We developed our campaign for the local and European elections, making major gains in both, in tandem with steady, and occasionally dramatic, gains in our support. Poll results are not votes, but we have begun to see signs that a major shift in the political landscape is possible. By September 2009, I felt confident enough about our progress to set out my objective of heading a Labour-led government. Although many commentators were sceptical about the claims we were making, Irish politics was increasingly becoming a three-horse race.

These changes brought new pressures. Ever since becoming a TD in 1989, I have kept my family life and my public life as separate as I can. As a TD, and even as a minister, it was possible to do this, but now, as party leader, and as a contender for the position of Taoiseach, there is a growing pressure on me to open up more about my background and home life. That is a side of politics with which I have never been comfortable, however. I have had requests to do celebrity-style interviews, but I'm afraid that it's just not me! My wife, Carol, is a huge personal support, but she has her own career, and does not wish to be in the public eye. Our three children, Gráinne, Oisín and Seán, all help out at election time in the constituency, but they have their own lives to lead. Carol, and indeed on occasion Gráinne, will sometimes accompany me to formal occasions, but mostly I do my political work alone.

At the same time, I can understand why people are interested in finding out more about someone who is asking for the privilege of leading the country. It's not just idle curiosity; it comes back to the issue of judgement. We are all products of where we come from, who we grew up with, and the people we have known at different points in our lives. And that, in turn, influences how we might react in a crisis.

That is why, when the idea for this book was put to me by Liberties Press, I agreed to do it. Their idea was simple: pick twelve people whom you admire, or who inspire you, or who have influenced you in some way, and write about them. I liked the idea, because it would give me a chance to write about people I have known and admired, and, through their stories, to talk about issues I care about, and values I hold dear. Values that I think are important to Ireland in meeting the challenges that confront our country. However, this is certainly not a biography or a political tract, and it's not a manifesto.

Of course, the first problem was to draw up a list of people to write about. This task proved to be far more difficult than I had expected. Many of those who were on the original list were great, inspiring figures from history, like James Connolly, or modern statesmen, like Nelson Mandela. As I thought about it more, however, and wrote and rewrote the list, it came to include fewer household names, and more people whom I have known personally. People who have had a direct influence on how I see the world, and on how I think about politics. In fact, of the twelve people I have written about in this book, there are only four whom I haven't actually met. Some, such as my grandmother, Ellen Gilmore, had an obvious influence on me. Others, such as Triona Dooney, were friends, but also individuals who stood out as examples of a type of person that, I think, has a lot to offer. Others, such as Joe Connolly, have little connection to politics, and simply reflect some of the things I am passionate about – in this case, Galway hurling!

This is not, as I say, a manifesto – although I have no doubt that some people will critique it on that basis. In fact, the charge that has been levelled against Labour recently – that we have 'no policies' – is somewhat ironic. Labour is, and always has been, a policy-driven party, and our approach to the economic crisis has been different to that of other parties. So, when people say you have 'no policies', perhaps what they mean is that they don't *like* your policies! We were the only party in the Dáil to vote against the blanket guarantee for the banks, and throughout the banking crisis, we have consistently put the interests of the taxpayer first. I believe that our position has been vindicated. More fundamentally, we have repeatedly made the point that Ireland has a jobs crisis as well as a banking crisis and a budget crisis, and that we need to fix all three. Labour has consistently put jobs at the top of the political agenda.

As the crisis has developed, we have had to rethink our policies, concentrating on three areas: jobs, reform and fairness. We have put forward numerous ideas on how to respond in the short term to the jobs crisis, particularly on how to provide hope and opportunity to those who are without work. We have also worked to build up a set of ideas that will promote growth in the Irish economy, focusing on how Ireland can create new jobs based on areas where we have natural advantages, from tourism to wind energy. I am strongly committed to the idea of a 'knowledge economy' but am increasingly frustrated by the way the term 'smart economy' is thrown around. Yes, we need to have a strong research base in Ireland, but not everyone is going to get a job working in a laboratory. The idea of a knowledge economy has to be translated into ideas for creating jobs across the country, at all skill levels.

The crisis we now face is perhaps the greatest in our history, but we have had economic crises before – at least three since the Second World War. It is appropriate that we ask fundamental questions about how we organise our affairs, to ensure that we prevent similar crises from occurring in the future. Real reform, however, will not be imposed from above. It has to come about through dialogue with the people of Ireland – which is the basis of my proposal for a constitutional convention. The Irish Constitution belongs to the people of Ireland, and reform must come from the people.

As the crisis has developed, there have been various attempts to demonise one group of people or another, so as to justify foisting the burden of the crisis onto them. I have resisted these efforts, because I fundamentally believe that we will get through our current difficulties only if we pull together. Over time, I have increasingly used the term 'One Ireland' to sum up this notion. This is based on the idea that fairness is a basic requirement for any solution to the current crisis, that as a country we must pull together to get through, and that, after we have done so, the Ireland we create is a fairer place, with real opportunities for our children.

As a country, I think we need to look again at who we are, where we have come from, and who we want to be. What kind of country do we want to create for our children? The answers to those questions come down to values. In the end, this is what politics is about: the values that you bring to bear on the decisions that you make. I hope that this book will shed some light on the experiences and values that keep me going.

Finally, I would like to extend my sincere thanks to Yseult Thornley, Liberties Press, Dr Colm O'Reardon, Jean O'Mahony, and my family for their help and support in its production.

Eamon Gilmore
October 2010

1

Ellen Gilmore

To everyone who knew her, she was Ellie. To her family, she was Granny Gilmore. But to my brother and me, she was always Nana. She lived with us in the family home, and was a constant presence in my early life. From her, more than anyone, I learned about where I was from and who my people were. She was a window not just into the history of our family but also into the history of a country that was experiencing the growing pains of independence.

Ellen Gilmore, my paternal grandmother, was born in Cloonruff, just outside Ballygar in east Galway. My grandfather made quite an impression on her the first time she saw him. She was in Ballygar one afternoon when she saw a man coming into town on horseback. His name was Edward Gilmore, but he was always known as Ned. They were married in 1918, in the run-up to the War of Independence; my grandfather had been involved in the independence movement. One of my most prized possessions is a beautiful set of china they were given as a wedding present by the local Sinn Féin club. Clearly it was precious to my grand-mother: it was hardly ever used. Now it sits, in pristine condition, in a special cabinet in the living room of my own home in Shankill, County Dublin. I like to think that I am minding it for the next generation.

After Ned and Ellie married, she went to live in the Gilmore family home in Lurgan, seven or eight miles away. We can trace the Gilmores back over four or five generations in that area. My grand-mother often related the family history to me: she told me that three Gilmore brothers and their families settled in the part of east Galway where I was born some generations later. If you look at the headstones in the village of Caltra, the earliest one with the Gilmore name is from 1812. The townland to which the Gilmores first moved was originally called Sean Cloch, according to my grand-mother, which is Irish for 'Old Stone'. When the three Gilmore brothers arrived, they renamed it Lurgan, because they had come from Lurgan in County Armagh. I often wondered about this, but many years later I found an old map, and discovered that she was right: the place had indeed been called Sean Cloch.

My grandmother came to have a very big presence in my child-hood, largely because of the tragedy which befell my family when I was a baby. She and my grandfather had five children, the oldest of whom, John Gilmore, was my father. He married my mother, Celia Concannon, in 1954. After their marriage, my parents lived in the family home in Lurgan. They had a small mixed farm, and my father worked at various things, including forestry, as well as on the farm. When I was just fourteen months old, and my mother was pregnant with my brother John, my father died suddenly. It was 8 June 1956, a sunny morning. After his breakfast, he played with me, then cycled off to work in the bog with a neighbour, John McHugh. As they were cycling along, my father suddenly fell off his bike. He had suffered a massive heart attack. He was just thirty-six.

My mother told me that he smoked heavily, but he was also incredibly strong. One of my uncles recalls him lifting a half-hundredweight with one hand and banging stakes in with it. He was not a tall man – only a little bit above my own height. Like many men of this generation, he probably put his body under immense physical strain, and didn't read the warning signs. One of my uncles remembers being with him, a few months before he died, when he complained of having pains in his chest. Yet he carried on, and then, out of the blue, he died. Suddenly, he was gone.

By this time, my grandmother was already a widow: my grandfather had died in 1948. Looking back, the sense of loss felt so keenly by both her and my mother must have brought them closer together. There was no time to dwell on these losses, however: there was simply too much to do. We all lived in the same house in Lurgan – a thatched cottage, with the surrounding farm. There was my grandmother, my mother, me, and my brother John. I also had a cousin, Nora Keary, who came to live with us; she soon came to be like an older sister to me and my brother. She was about thirteen or fourteen at the time, and had come to provide company and support for my mother.

The farm covered about thirty acres, and was scattered. There were a number of good fields quite close to the house, but the ones further away were quite marshy and were used mainly for grazing. We all worked; from a very early age, my brother and I were out on the land. We also learned how to cook. Everybody did everything, as the need arose.

My grandmother was a talented and passionate gardener, and she was most content when she was working in the garden. I can still see where everything was in the flower garden at the front of that house, as though I were looking at a photo. There were fabulous roses, wall-flowers and dahlias. It was utterly beautiful, almost idyllic. At the rear there was a vegetable garden, with several types of apple trees – for eating or cooking. She grew potatoes, carrots and a variety of onions and cabbages; we helped her with them. Far up in one corner was the rhubarb patch, which produced wonderful fruit. Rhubarb is still my favourite filling for a pie or crumble.

All of our vegetables were home-produced, and we learned how to conserve and keep them. They would be put into a pit: they would keep through the winter and then provide the seed for the next crop in the new year. My grandmother was also very successful when it came to rearing fowl. Eggs were something we sold, not something we bought. That was part of the economy of the farm. In fact, eggs were probably our most regular source of income.

We had cows that produced the milk, and we used that in our kitchen. We skimmed it and kept the cream; some of this was churned and made into butter. What was left after churning was used as animal feed for the sheep and cattle. We also grew oats and wheat, and my grandmother and my mother baked their own bread.

The killing of the pig was a ritual on the farm – as it was on many farms at the time. A neighbour who had some skill at this would arrive, surreptitiously observed by John and me: we were officially supposed to be sheltered from witnessing the slaughter! From the pig came the pudding and the sausages, the pork joints and the bacon. There were no refrigerators then, so it was distributed amongst the neighbours. I would go from house to house on my bicycle, distributing the parcels. This would be reciprocated by the neighbours when they killed their own pigs. The bulk of the pig was then cured as bacon and stored in wooden boxes made specifically for the purpose. I remember it all well; at a push, I'd probably still be able to do it.

It was a naturally, unselfconsciously self-sufficient life. Almost everything we ate came from the land around us. Good crop management and rotation preserved the nutrients in the soil. I have no memory of us ever buying any vegetables or milk until I was in my teens, and we had moved house. These days, organic products are all the rage, but we forget that not much more than forty years ago, and for centuries before that, everything we grew was organic.

My grandmother was a wellspring of local knowledge. On top of numerous delicious recipes, she had cures for all kinds of ailments. She possessed a vast, folkloric knowledge of local plants and the remedies they could provide. She could have written her own book, filled with wisdom stretching back two centuries. The Ireland that she was able to tell me about was one in which not much had changed for hundreds of years. She drew on her own heritage, on skills handed down from generation to generation, in her garden, and in how she related to nature. Just by looking at an orange glow in the sky in the evening, she would be able to predict the next day's weather. Yet her remarkable life straddled two very different Irelands: she also used to look up at the sky and, seeing a plane, wonder aloud: 'How do they stay up there?' For me, she provided an endlessly rich perspective on the past.

She was a new bride during the War of Independence. My grandfather took part in what were known locally as the 'cattle drives' – an attempt by small farmers to have the landholdings of larger farmers broken up and divided out between them. They would drive the stock of the big farmers off the land, and drive their own stock on to it, occupying farms. Once, their home was raided by the Black and Tans. They searched the house, but were unaware that their quarry was hiding outside under her cabbages!

My grandmother also had vivid memories of the period imme-diately after the Civil War. She would often talk about the people who were 'johnny-come-lately' Fianna Fáilers. According to her, few people in the local area had opposed the Treaty during the Civil War – but many people changed their position when it became clear that Fianna Fáil's star was in the ascendant. I suppose this was meant to highlight the constancy of my own family's support for Fianna Fáil. Our family was steeped in Fianna Fáil, and we were enthusiastic supporters of Éamon de Valera. At that time, you were either Fianna

Fáil or Fine Gael. If you were a Labour person, you were considered a Communist – something to be spoken of only in hushed tones. Except, of course, for Noël Browne, who was well regarded, particularly by my grandmother. Browne was seen as a hero, almost on a par with de Valera, for his role in eradicating TB from Ireland. However, for most of the family, their loyalty to Fianna Fáil never wavered: when my mother remarried in the late 1960s, she and my stepfather, Tommy Keane, were both active party members.

It was from my mother that I learned about Ireland during the Second World War. The war loomed large in my mother's memory, perhaps because it had determined the course of her own life: she had left school at fifteen, with the intention of emigrating to the United States – a decision which was thwarted by the outbreak of war.

My mother came from a place called Windfield, in the parish of Skehana, about ten or twelve miles from Caltra. Her father, Thomas Concannon, was an agent for the Jamesons – the local landlords, and the family that made the eponymous whiskey. Her mother, Sara Maguire, had emigrated to the United States, but she later returned and married Thomas. There were three daughters: Rita, Katie, and my mother Celia (or Sadie, as she came to be known) in the middle.

Most of the stories my mother told about the war dealt with rationing: how difficult it was to get things like tyres for bicycles and batteries for radios. She also talked about how hard it became to travel. Instead of going to America, she had to stay at home and help with the work on the farm. My mother was self-taught and ultimately very well educated, but she always regretted the fact that she had not had more formal schooling. Therefore, her primary ambition for my brother and me was that we would be educated. It was her passion, and she showed great determination in achieving her goal. The primary school which she chose for us had a reputation for preparing pupils for scholarships and exams. In the absence of free second-level education, a scholarship was the only way that someone from a family of modest means could get the Leaving Certificate. Sure enough, at the age of twelve I started, with the help of scholarships, as a boarder in Garbally College in Ballinasloe.

When I was thirteen, at the end of my first year in secondary school, we moved house. It was 1968, and the Land Commission was doing a lot of good work in rural Ireland, consolidating people's holdings and working to improve living conditions. The post-independence drive to redistribute land – for which my grandfather had agitated – had resulted in a situation where there were tens of thousands of small, unproductive farms, with scattered pieces added on through successive Land Acts. Our own farm, for example, was in four pieces. It is somewhat ironic, then, that it was through attempts to reverse the damage of this policy that my family ended up moving to a new house, and its accompanying thirty-seven acres, in Lislea, a little closer to Caltra.

The move was a source of tension between my mother and my grandmother. Moving from the traditional home place was traumatic for my grandmother: she had married into the house as a young woman and had raised her children there. It also meant leaving her beloved garden. She resisted, but in the end, of course, she came with us, swapping her place in front of the fire in the old house for a permanent spot beside the Stanley range in the new home. More positively for my mother, the move meant that all of her land would be together, and she would have a modern house. And more importantly, it was to be a fresh start, away from a place that held painful memories for her. As it turned out, she *did* make a fresh start: within a year and a half of our moving into the new house, she had remarried. Tommy Keane, my mother's second husband, was a local man; he was employed by the county council as a road worker, and also ran a part-time hackney service.

Like almost every other family at the time, we were touched by emigration. Shortly after we moved into the new house, a stranger pulled up to the gate. He was American, and told me that he was looking for Edward Gilmore. I assumed that he was looking for my uncle Eddie – who was the local travel agent, among other things. When I eventually realised that he was looking for my grandfather, I said to him: 'Well, you're a bit late!' I brought him and his wife inside to see my grandmother – and was struck by the incongruousness of these two big, colourful Americans in our modest kitchen. She had difficulty capturing what they were saying because of their accent but, with me acting as translator, she established what they were looking for. She sent me to fetch an old photograph – a picture, taken in America, of a man and a woman with a child, who was probably about two or three years old. When she handed the photo to the visitor, he began to cry. The child was himself, and the mother was my grandfather's sister, who had emigrated to the United States in the early 1900s. For whatever reason, they had lost all contact with the family until this man showed up, armed only with the knowledge that his mother had a brother called Edward Gilmore, and that he came from County Galway. That man's name was John Dalton. He had been an engineer with the NASA space programme. When he returned to the United States, he sent me a gift of a monthly subscription to *National Geographic* magazine.

My uncle Martin, my father's younger brother, emigrated to England and lived all his life in Coventry, where he worked in the car industry. My uncle Hugh emigrated, at a later stage, to Birmingham. They came back on holidays in the summer for two weeks every year, and were very supportive of my mother, giving her a lot of advice over the years. My aunt Katie emigrated to Boston, and many of my cousins and step-cousins still live in parts of the UK, USA and Australia. Such a widely spread extended family was always part of growing up in Ireland.

At the height of the boom, a significant amount of my time doing constituency work was spent trying to help new immigrants: at one stage, they accounted for about half of the people who were coming to my clinic. They usually came to see me with problems regarding their documentation or their status. Only those with Irish or British citizenship are allowed to vote in general elections: so one might reasonably ask why an elected representative would take on what can be quite complex cases. For me, it's a question of reciprocity that crosses generations and continents. For every immigrant who came into my clinic looking to me for help, there would have been an Irish emigrant approaching a Democrat politician in Boston or a Labour politician in London or Australia for the same reason. Now that the wheel of history had turned, and we were a country that people were coming to rather than emigrating from, it was our turn to return the favour, as I saw it. Now, because of the recession, another generation of Irish people are facing emigration. The wheel has turned again.

*

Ours was a close-knit household, but it also rested on the shoulders of a much wider community of friends, neighbours and family members. That support is one of the abiding memories of my child-hood. There was a steady stream of uncles and cousins coming to help on the farm, perhaps to some extent taking the place of my father. My two uncles, Eddie and Hugh, one or the other of them, would come to the house every Sunday and take us out on treats – usually day trips to Galway or the seaside. My aunt Mary-Ann, my grandmother's last child, was also a constant visitor. She lives in County Roscommon. Her husband, Andrew, used to come and do some of the farm work with his brother John. Then there was my aunt Rita, her husband, John Paul, and the older cousins; they all regularly came to help out. Even though my father was dead, in another sense he was a constant presence, because my mother and grandmother talked about him so often. He was missed.

By all accounts he was a very witty man. My memory of him is of somebody who was smiling all the time: he was smiling in all the photographs we had of him.

Our house seemed always to be full when I was growing up, with visitors constantly coming and going, having something to eat, or a bottle of stout. It was like a restaurant, with meals constantly being prepared. Years later, watching the classic French film *Manon des Sources*, which evokes that blend of farm work and eating, I realised that this is a universal aspect of rural life. I associate our house with the endless preparing and enjoying of food, with lots of people gathered around the table. Ours was a house filled with laughter, but there was always the vacant chair.

One of the big annual events in the locality was the threshing. There was one, enormous threshing machine which visited every townland; after the harvest, every farm used it to separate the corn from the straw. We took it in turns to help, because no one family could manage to do it all on their own. The term that best describes this is the Irish *an meitheal*. It comes from the idea of the village collective, where the village assembles to help gather each other's crops, in order to maximise their harvest. The concept of *an meitheal* is familiar to Irish people, even those who did not grow up in a rural community. At its heart is the way in which solidarity between individual strengthens the entire community. When I gave a speech to the Labour Party conference in Kilkenny in 2008, as the consequences of the economic crash were beginning to be felt by every household in the country, it was that term – *an meitheal* – that came back to me. It was clear to me that Ireland, as a community, would have to pull together in order to get out of the crisis: that no single group, no matter how blameless, or how culpable, for the crisis, and regardless of whether they were involved with the public or the private sector, was going to provide a magic solution. Rather, we *all* were the solution, but only if we embraced that part of our heritage – the best of our national psyche – that manifested itself in *an meitheal.*

While all this activity was going on at home, Ellie was sitting beside the fire and holding court for the parades of people who would stream through our kitchen to see her. She was liked – and loved – by so many. One night, when she was eighty-three, she watched the movie *Mutiny on the Bounty*, went to bed and never woke up.

Aside from my mother, my grandmother is the person in my life who most influenced me. She was like a second parent; she was my court of appeal – and usually found in my favour! She exercised great authority in the house and could often be very sharp. However, in many ways it was the classic stuff of grannies, and, as with other grannies the length and breadth of Ireland, it never seemed to impinge on her popularity. She had a voracious interest in current affairs, history and politics, which she would often discuss with me. Looking back, those conversations in front of the range were to lay the foundations for my own interest in politics.

My grandmother was a prism through which I could glimpse centuries of history. She was, herself, living history. Because of her,

I came to realise that I was only one link in a chain stretching through many generations – that I was part of a continuum. Through her, I came to know where I had come from.

2

Father Joe Cassidy

We can all remember a teacher who made a strong impact on us when we were young, and affected the rest of our lives. For me, Father Joe Cassidy is that teacher. He taught me English and Civics at secondary school, in Garbally College, Ballinasloe, County Galway, but his impact on me extended well beyond those subjects. He was a marvellous teacher and an inspirational figure.

I first came across Joe Cassidy before I went to Garbally. I remember a meeting in the parish hall in Caltra, which was convened to discuss 'Saving the West'. It was sometime in the mid-1960s; I would have been about eleven. The speaker was to have been the founder of the 'Save the West' campaign, a priest from Glencolmcille, Father McDyer, who had founded the Errigal Co-operative in County Donegal. His co-operative had been so successful that it had spread beyond his native county. He was now leading a movement, along with other priests and local organisations, with the aim of bringing people together and establishing more co-operatives. These efforts were all taking place under the umbrella of the Save the West campaign.

By the time of the meeting in Caltra, he had become quite famous. I'm not sure why I was there: I suspect that our primary teacher probably rustled up as many of the senior pupils as possible in order to fill the hall. However, Father McDyer didn't show up; he was replaced by a Father Joe Cassidy, who seemed a very different kind of priest from the ones I was used to. He was speaking about things which were radical for Ireland in the 1960s: the importance of people organising in co-operatives, being united and working together for the benefit of their communities. That day, he sparked an interest in these things in me, and left a big impression.

The next time I saw him, I was sitting the scholarship exam in Garbally College in Ballinasloe. He was a teacher there, taking his turn supervising the hall. After I became a boarder in Garbally, he was a strong presence in my life for the next five years. Ultimately, his influence would stretch far beyond those five years of schooling.

I started in Garbally College in 1967. This was the year that free second-level schooling was introduced, but, as I have said, at that time, the only way that a boy from my background could get to secondary school was by winning a scholarship to one of the boarding schools. These schools were all fee-paying: the fees for Garbally then were £90 a year for boarders, and the cost of things like sports equipment, books and laundry brought the total expense to around £120 a year. This was a lot of money then, and was certainly beyond my family's means. At the time, there was a county council scholarship worth £80, which I was awarded. But as individual schools offered scholarships too, I also sat the scholarship exam in Garbally, which was worth £50. Ultimately, I was awarded both. However, the college's rule was that you could take only one of the scholarships. My mother had a meeting with the president of the college, Father Dermot Byrne, to negotiate, and he agreed to combine the two. I never learned why he agreed to make an exception in my case, but it is something for which I will always be profoundly grateful. I was able to attend Garbally as a boarder, and my mother did not have to pay any bills during my time there.

Our education – that of my brother John and me – was extremely important to my mother. Before I went to Garbally, I had already had a very good primary education in a two-teacher school in Caltra. Although Caltra National School was somewhat further away than the nearest, and more convenient, primary school, my mother chose it because it had the best reputation for preparing pupils for scholarships. She was determined that John and I would have the educational opportunities which she herself had not. No other child in our neighbourhood in Lurgan was going to Caltra, so she bought a carrier for her bicycle, popped me into it every morning, and cycled me to school until I was old enough to make the trip on my own.

The principal of Caltra National School was a man called Michael Hogan, who had a passionate interest in the Irish language and Irish music. Mary Kilcommins was our teacher up to second class. She later married Pat O'Dowd (I served the Mass at their wedding) and moved to Dublin, where she became the principal of St Kevin's Primary School in Sallynoggin – coincidentally, in the constituency I ended up serving as a public representative.

Caltra was not an all-Irish school, but all the teaching was done through Irish, apart from English class. We even spoke Irish passing the ball in the playground. It was a complete immersion in Irish, but only as far as the school gate; this was an English-speaking area, and we spoke English at home.

Like hundreds of small rural schools today, the school at Caltra was home to several class groups which had to be conducted simultaneously. Both teachers were great motivators, just as many of the teachers in Garbally later proved to be. They encouraged pupils to learn. We learned how to learn, and we were encouraged to read. The county council's mobile library came once a week. We borrowed Dickens, or one of the classics, and when the library returned the next week, we borrowed another one. Books, and reading, were an important part of my primary-school experience – and were to become an indelible part of my second-level experience too. I had a very good grounding by the time I went to Garbally College at the age of twelve.

Garbally was then, and still is, owned by the diocese of Clonfert and run by Diocesan priests. Back then, about half the teachers were priests and half were lay teachers. The student population was about 400 boys, of whom 180 or so were boarders. The college was housed in the big landlord's house in Ballinasloe, which had once been the home of the Clancarty family. In 1922, the diocese of Clonfert purchased Garbally from the trustees for the Earls of Clancarty in order to establish a secondary school. However, it retained all the trappings of an old landlord's house: there were beautiful gardens and woodlands. I remember particularly the long walkway, with an obelisk at one end and thirty-nine steps at the other. Whenever I see the film *The Thirty-nine Steps*, I always think of that place.

The history of the house was a rich source of school legends. One particular story, which sent a chill up the spine of the boarders, concerned a long-gone Lord Clancarty, who had thrown his wife over the banisters to a bloody death. The story went that after he had thrown her over the banisters, he went down, picked up the body, and dragged her upstairs, along the corridor and into a bed-room (now a dormitory), where he buried her in the wall. Sure enough, when you lifted the carpet along the main stairway, there was a stain running up the stairs and into dormitory number seven. The unfortunate Lady Clancarty was said to have haunted this par-ticular dormitory ever since. Every means of washing had been employed over the centuries, but no one could remove the bloody stain that led to the dormitory.

Father Cassidy taught my class English from second year, all the way through to the Leaving Certificate. A great communicator, he imbued in us a love of reading and literature. I was quite shy when I went to secondary school, and initially I had great difficulty following the classes. In primary school, we had done everything through Irish; the sudden transition to English proved very difficult for me. Things like mathematical terms and arithmetic were all new, because I had only ever learned them in Irish. I even counted in Irish.

Of all my teachers at Garbally, Father Cassidy was the one I got to know best. He was responsible for organising the school opera; despite the fact that I couldn't sing a note, I managed to play parts in it. He also ran one of the school magazines, *The Fountain*, which was named after another vestige of the college's Anglo-Irish past – a large fountain at the back of the school.

While he had overall control of the magazine, Father Cassidy in effect handed over the running of *The Fountain* to the students. This was an extraordinary degree of autonomy for a teacher to give to students in a secondary school at that time. The magazine was also very democratic in the way in which it was managed. At the start of every school year, two pupils were elected as the editorial board by the senior students. I was elected in my third year, and worked on the magazine until I left the school. We worked as a team, with some supervision – and, it must be said, the odd grammatical correction – from Father Cassidy. However, the aim of *The Fountain* was to enable the students to express themselves – to say their piece about topical or interesting subjects. Past pupils were invited to contribute to the magazine. During my time, the novelist John Broderick regularly wrote for the magazine; Eugene Waters – or Eoghan Ó Tuairisg, as he was known in Irish – was also a contributor. The magazine came out once a year, and was professionally printed. Funds were raised in the form of contributions from past pupils, elicited by means of regular begging letters.

Looking back, the freedom we were given by Father Cassidy was probably his way of developing our character. What impressed me about him was the confidence with which he delegated responsibility to others. It was an approach to leadership that actively cultivated independence, teamwork, and the strengths and talents of others.

Father Cassidy's other great contribution to student life at Garbally was the regular debating competitions he organised. He was fond of reminding us that 'Free speech is great, but it's not much good if you can't use it'.

I still remember my first experience of speaking in public. The subject was the GAA ban on members playing 'foreign' sports, which was then in force. This was a big issue in Garbally because it was a rugby-playing school located in Ballinasloe, a stronghold of Gaelic football and hurling. A school like Garbally, which was strong in both rugby and hurling, could have found itself in a rather invidious position. Instead, as with many an Irish problem, an Irish solution was found: you played rugby using your English name and hurling using your Irish name!

At this time, in the late 1960s, there were motions going to the GAA congress to remove the ban. Every pupil was required to speak in front of the class, and I was told to make the case for removing the ban. I remember being petrified at the prospect – positively sick with terror. It is one of my worst memories from school, and yet it probably helped me develop a talent which was to be of some use to me later in life! In time, speaking in public came more easily to me, and after an outbreak of mumps laid waste to most of my class-mates, I found myself on our class debating team. Some things never change, though, and I still feel that knot of anticipation just before I get up to speak in the Dáil – or anywhere else, for that matter. Perhaps that sprinkling of nerves is nature's way of keeping us sharp.

Joe Cassidy – or Hoppy, as he was known – was a truly outstand-ing teacher. The love that I have now of reading, literature and the-atre I learned from him. I know that this is something I share with other people who were lucky enough to be his pupils. However, I think the most significant thing I learned from him was how to speak in public and, crucially, how to find the confidence to do so. Not only did he bring me from a relatively basic level of English, when I arrived in the school, to a very good standard by the time I left, but he was also an enthusiast for good writing, for which he had a devoted appreciation. He was someone who impressed on me the power of language – to persuade, to inspire, and, most of all, to give flight to an idea. His was a gift that I have drawn on all my life, from my days in student politics to Leader's Questions in Dáil Éireann.

Later, after I left the school, I kept in regular contact with him. That friendship and contact were important to me – so much so that when Carol and I married, he performed the wedding cere-mony. The first phone call I get after every general election, congrat-ulating me, is from Joe Cassidy. When I was first elected to the Dáil, in 1989, I remember that he called me and said: 'Well done, ladeen [he always referred to the pupils as 'ladeens'], you'll be there now for as long as Blaney.' Neil Blaney, a Donegal TD, was first elected to the

Dáil in 1948 and, at that time, was its longest-serving member.

For me, Father Cassidy embodied the ethos of my secondary school. That ethos was about cultivating independence, not simply obedience. We were encouraged to think for ourselves. It was a place where swimming against the tide was encouraged, not suppressed – a philosophy which has shaped my thinking about education. Put simply, I believe that education is the great liberator. It is the key that unlocks a person's potential and gives them the tools to craft their own future.

I was lucky enough to attend a wonderful secondary school, and to go on to university. Donogh O'Malley's education reforms were implemented in the late 1960s. We only need to look at the boom years of the 1990s to see what can happen when you liberate the pent-up talent of a whole generation. The Celtic Tiger was made possible by the existence of a critical mass of people who had bene-fited from the opening up of secondary education beyond the ranks of the well-off and the odd scholarship student.

It is unimaginable to us now that a child leaving primary school at the age of eleven or twelve would face the prospect of having to work for a living if his or her parents could not afford to pay school fees. Politically, no one would dare to suggest that, even in the midst of a profound economic crisis, fees for secondary schools should be reintroduced. I believe that Irish people instinctively understand the value of education – the freedom, the dignity, the independence it affords, and the role it plays in developing our society and our economy.

It is interesting, then, that free access to third-level education, introduced by a Labour Minister for Education, Niamh Bhreathnach, in 1995, has been the subject of such criticism by some in the media, and in academic circles. Yet, if we take the view that education is a right – as most people believe – when does that right become conditional on ability to pay? Up to 1995, once you sat your Leaving Certificate, your automatic right to an education stopped there. If you were lucky enough to have well-off parents who could write your fees off against their tax bill, or if one of your parents worked in a university, you could proceed as far as your talents would take you. However, if your parents were PAYE workers on a modest wage, you could go only as far as they could afford. Perhaps that meant that you would be able to go to college – but only if your other siblings did not.

I am not going to rehash here the arguments for abolishing third-level fees in 1995 – how it cost the same as was being lost to the Exchequer in tax-covenanting; how it was never regarded as a panacea for deep-seated educational disadvantage. Rather, I want to talk about why education matters, and why access to it should be universal.

In 1967, when Donogh O'Malley introduced free post-primary education, a second-level education was often enough to advance in work, to increase your income, and so to improve the prospects for your family. Today, a Leaving Certificate is usually the minimum qualification needed to get a job. For higher-paid jobs, even a good undergraduate degree might not be enough: as many parents will tell you, these days a Master's degree is considered an entry-level qualification.

Education is valuable. It is valuable to the individual in ways we could never quantify: a lifelong love of poetry, or a fascination with geography, or the private joy of being able to play the piano. And education is valuable in ways we *can* quantify, such as a person's earning power. However, it is also valuable to us as a people: it enables us to develop new products and services, create jobs, attract foreign companies, build bridges and roads, and treat people when they are sick. That is why social democrats do not believe that education should be rationed, or that it is only for an elite. There were many practical reasons for abolishing fees in 1995 – not least the value to the economy of expanding our base of third-level graduates, much as had been done by Donogh O'Malley for second-level education in 1967 – but at the heart of it was a refusal to say to another generation of talented young people: 'Thus far shall you go, and no farther.'

Those who argue that fees should be reintroduced because rich people's children go to university are wilfully missing the point. When education is rationed, the children of very well-off people get to go regardless. Putting up barriers to accessing education affects the majority of people from middle- and lower-income families – the people who benefited the most by the abolition of tuition fees. Perhaps that is why I have yet to hear a parent on a modest wage make the argument for reintroducing third-level fees. Making education a right of citizenship from preschool to third level – not a right that is conditional on your income – benefits all of us, as individuals and as a community. It is an investment that repays itself many times over, in the quality of our society, and in the sustainability of our economy.

Even before I went to primary school, I could read and write: my mother taught me. Literacy is the most basic and most important skill our schools teach. As my colleague Ruairi Quinn says: 'You learn to read so you can read to learn.' Literacy is the key that unlocks all subsequent education, but it is also vital for following an independent life, and when it comes to exercising your democratic rights. Poor literacy makes you more likely to leave school early, more likely to experience poverty, more likely to work for low pay, and more likely to spend time in prison. It also means that your children are more likely to experience the same problems.

In Ireland today, one in ten children has very poor literacy – the same proportion as in 1980. In some disadvantaged schools, that number is one in every three children. More worryingly still, one in eight fifteen-year-olds don't have the literacy skills they need to progress in education, or to meet the demands of most modern jobs. The primary-school class of 2010 is the first generation of Irish children not to have a better standard of literacy than their parents did.

If we want to improve overall literacy rates for the first time in thirty years, we need to be more radical in our approach. Improving literacy does not cost a lot of money, or require high-tech equipment. All the evidence on raising literacy standards says that we already have the most important resource in every classroom already: teachers. However, we have to improve how they teach literacy and how long they teach it for, and to make every principal responsible for raising reading standards in their school. The Irish education system has always been fortunate in attracting good, motivated teachers; if we want to see real change, we need to give them the skills to be even better.

What actually goes on in the classroom – the most important part of education – is strangely missing from much of the debate about education in Ireland. There is a lot of attention paid to what we put into education, but not a lot about what we get out of it. One of the things I cherish most about my secondary-school education is the variety of what we were taught. We learnt not just in the classroom but also on the playing field, on the stage, and out in the community, where we volunteered. The focus of my school was on the whole child – on creating rounded individuals.

The Leaving Certificate, which my youngest son, Seán, is about to sit, is not much different from the exam I sat, yet there is a huge chasm between the world I grew up in, and the one Seán will inherit. It strikes me that the needs of today's generation of young people, in light of the huge technological advances that have taken place and the transformation of the workplace which has occurred, should be reflected better in what is taught in the curriculum, and also *how* it is taught. Many aspects of the Leaving Certificate are good, but the way it is currently structured, and the intensity of the final two weeks of exams, can have a deadening effect on the kind of skills which can't be measured by a three-hour exam, but which are nonetheless increasingly important. Stretching those exams over the final two years of school, breaking some subjects into shorter modules, and cultivating the kind of skills that facilitate learning throughout life would be a start in broadening the benefits of second-level education beyond memory and stamina. Our goal must be to create a nation of learners, not just cogs in the wheel.

The pluralist philosophy adopted by my own second-level teachers was all the more remarkable for the fact that it was a diocesan school, whose stated primary objective was to recruit young men for the priesthood. Ireland's long history and strong tradition of religious involvement in education has become more complicated and more contentious over the past few decades. While the majority of people are still happy to call themselves Catholic, there are now more people of no religion than there are members of the next-biggest faith, and attendance at religious services has fallen off dramatically. Ireland, long a country which exported its people, became a country of net immigration from the mid-1990s. Today, more than one in ten people living here were not born in Ireland, and with them has come a wider variety of faiths and cultures. All of which begs the question whether a school system that is mostly denominational, and dominated by the Catholic Church, is still suitable.

Some would favour a complete end to religious involvement in education. The state pays for the upkeep of buildings, for the bills and for the teachers – so why shouldn't they take over the management of the schools too? However, this view forgets one of the most important assets of our school system: parents, and the time they volunteer helping to manage schools. You cannot put a price on the involvement of parents in the running of a school – something which is common to every community in Ireland. Indeed, other countries, such as Britain and the US, are trying to enact reforms to achieve precisely that. Educating the next generation is a unique partnership between the state, parents and educators. All three need to be part of any reforms designed to make our school system more inclusive, and more responsive to modern Irish society.

Some of the most active debate about the role of the Catholic Church in Irish education is coming from the church itself. Archbishop Diarmuid Martin has acknowledged that a situation where the Catholic Church controls more than 90 percent of schools is out of step with the reality of modern Ireland. It is the government that has been slowest to respond to change. My Labour Party colleague Ruairi Quinn has proposed the setting up of a national forum to discuss, in policy terms, what the future of patronage should be for Irish schools. This forum would invite all those with an interest in education – religious leaders, teachers and parents – to have their say, and to find an agreed way forward.

I believe that the solution to this challenge will ultimately be found in the communities that schools serve, if those communities are given a democratic voice. After all, it is up to parents to decide what type of ethos the school in which their child is educated should have. However, in many communities, particularly outside the cities, that choice is more a theoretical one than a practical one, because all the local primary schools are Catholic. If we re-imagine our local schools as part of a network, serving the wider community, then maybe we could start to ask what the right mix of ethos is, to reflect that community. Once we do that, we could give parents a vote in what they think that mix should be. Perhaps all the schools would remain Catholic; perhaps some would become Educate Together, or VEC. The important thing is that parents have more control over the management of the school, whatever its ethos.

It would not be difficult to facilitate a more democratic, pluralist system. Instead of school infrastructure belonging to the patron (usually the Catholic Church) but being managed centrally by the Department of Education, it makes sense to vest school buildings, and the responsibility for their planning and upkeep, in a local education board or authority. I hate to see school buildings sold, and apartments or shopping centres built in their place. Of course, the religious orders have made a valuable contribution to the Irish education system over the years, and their elderly members have a right to a secure and dignified retirement. However, it is imperative that school buildings are kept in education, so that they can be 'recycled' to meet the needs of a changing community.

As well as being able to assess the provision of school buildings and facilities for the wider community – for example, where schools could share laboratories or playing pitches – a local educational authority could manage a democratic vote on the ethos of local schools. It could even coordinate the sharing of teachers between schools, so that schools could afford to broaden the subject choices they offer to pupils. These local education authorities should themselves be democratically elected, as happens in many other countries, such as the US.

Whatever we decide together, as a people, regarding the future of our school system, the two most important changes have to be greater transparency and more democratic management. With these comes trust, and nothing is more important to a parent than that.

The other major challenge facing us today is the need to upskill our workforce, in particular those who find themselves out of work. We have to do everything in our power to avoid the emergence of long-term unemployment; maintaining or improving people's skills while they are on the dole is a crucial part of that. With over four hundred thousand of our fellow men and women on the live register, we need nothing less than a war effort to ensure that they are ready to take advantage of the economic recovery, when it comes.

This is particularly true of lower-skilled workers. High wages on construction sites were a magnet for young men during the boom years, encouraging them to leave school before taking the Leaving Cert. At the height of the boom, more than eighty thousand construction workers had only a Junior Certificate education, or less. Now there are more than a hundred thousand people who previously worked in construction-related industries looking for jobs. The construction industry in Ireland will never again reach those artificially inflated heights, when one in every eight men in the labour force was employed in the sector. Unless we make a concerted effort to retrain these men to work in other, more sustainable jobs, they will be at risk of a lifetime of poor employment prospects or joblessness. The same is true of other men and women, whose skills do not match the needs of an increasingly knowledge-based economy.

Not every person in Ireland is going to work in a lab in a white coat; that is not what I mean by a knowledge economy. A knowledge economy is one where every job, at every level, and in every sector, is more knowledge-intensive then before. Twenty years ago, if you could type on a computer, you were an IT specialist. Now, you need to know how to use a computer in almost every job, from nursing to working at a supermarket checkout.

We have our work cut out for us. One in four people already in the Irish workforce needs to move up a skill level if we are going to continue to attract investment and expand employment. I believe that we can do this, if we make it a national priority. We need to think laterally too: could some people who find themselves on the dole use their skills to train others? Could carpenters help train people up in retrofitting a house to make it more energy-efficient? Could unemployed engineers put their mathematical knowledge to use in our schools? Finding yourself out of work is often an isolating and demoralising experience; we need to show people that there is light at the end of the tunnel, that training or acquiring new skills is one of the ways of getting there, and that their huge wealth of knowledge and life experience is still valuable.

Recently, I was invited back to Garbally College to speak at their graduation ceremony. It is not an easy time to be graduating from school – jobs, and indeed any good news on the economy, are thin on the ground. Yet when I met the young class of 2010, and their proud parents, I felt hopeful. This generation certainly faces a difficult challenge, but they are by no means the first generation of Irish people to do so. And like others before them, they will not be found wanting.

*

Father Joe Cassidy went on to become president of Garbally College, Bishop of Clonfert and Archbishop of Tuam. I was honoured to attend his installation as bishop. Throughout the 1980s, he was the official spokesperson for the Catholic hierarchy. We were on different sides of many of the public controversies during that time – the abortion referenda, the divorce referendum and the legalisation of contraception – but that never interfered with or dampened our friendship and mutual respect.

I always felt that Joe Cassidy expressed the conservative view of the Catholic hierarchy on these contentious issues with compassion and with great respect for those of us who did not share the viewpoint of the Catholic Church. This sensitive way of communicating stands in marked contrast to the dogmatic tone struck by some of those in the more conservative Catholic press, who are quick to label as 'anti-Catholic' and 'anti-religion' those who question some of their orthodoxies on school governance and other social issues.

Apart from his influence on me as a school pupil, Joe Cassidy was also helpful to me in another way – and in a way for which he never sought acknowledgement. He was hugely supportive towards my mother, and helped her to understand – or at least accept – some of the unorthodox political choices which I had made. Campaigning for social change in a conservative Ireland was sometimes uncomfortable. My late mother was deeply religious, and my radical views, and the path I took in politics, did not always sit comfortably with her loyalty to the Catholic Church, or with her political affiliation. Archbishop Cassidy called in on her from time to time. I think he at least reassured her that I was not necessarily heading for eternal damnation! I was greatly comforted when, although he was in declining health, he came to celebrate her funeral Mass in Caltra in November 2007.

3

Triona Dooney

Triona Dooney was one of the best friends that Carol and I have ever had. We were all friends from college and our children called her Auntie Triona.

Following my Leaving Certificate, I went to University College Galway (now NUIG) in 1972 on a student grant. I wanted to study economics and psychology, which UCG was offering as a new degree course. However, I quickly learned that college was not just about study; it was also about making friends.

Making friends in college is done by osmosis. You find yourself part of a social circle, and are never quite sure when or how you first met: you just know that a commonality of interests binds you all together. All I can recall is that I found myself in a social milieu which included Carol Hanney, with whom I fell in love, and Triona Dooney, who became a lifelong friend. There were, of course, many other friends.

Triona was a couple of years ahead of us, studying English and

French – the same subjects as Carol. Certain student houses tended to be magnets for parties, for late-night conversations, and for just hanging out. Two houses which Triona shared were centres of such social and intellectual gatherings: one on Newcastle Road, and the other at New Docks.

New Docks was on the waterfront, around the corner from Long Walk, where Carol was living when we started going out. The local pub was McDonagh's on Merchant's Row, which was owned by a veteran of the Merchant Navy, known as Sailor McDonagh. Sailor's was host to an eclectic mix of seafarers, local Galway characters, university staff – some of whom might have successfully auditioned for Michael Caine's part in *Educating Rita* – and those of us who hung around the house in New Docks. Opening hours at McDonagh's were somewhat flexible. After official closing time, the ritual for gaining entry was to knock at the door, go around the corner, wait for Sailor to open the upstairs window, declare who you were, and wait to be admitted, discreetly.

Sailor McDonagh's was at the heart of the docks area, just past the Spanish Arch. It was a magical place: we loved hanging around and watching the boats coming in from all kinds of places – and meeting people from all over the world. The seafaring history of the place was all-pervasive: around the Spanish Arch you got a real sense of what Galway would have been like as a port back in the sixteenth century; you could almost see the Spanish vessels coming in to harbour carrying their cargoes of wine. Columbus is said to have come to Galway to find sailors to accompany him to travel to the New World.

Our friends at the time were mainly engineering and medical students. One was Brian Gibbons – who also lived in New Docks for a time. His father, Dr Hugh Gibbons, was a Fianna Fáil TD in Roscommon. Later in life, Brian practised medicine in Wales, was elected as a Labour member of the Welsh Assembly, and served for a number of years there as Minister for Health and Social Services.

Triona was a great thinker, and was deeply political, eventually becoming vice-president of the Workers' Party. She was one of the most widely read people I have ever known. She read literature, history, politics – everything. After she finished her degree, she decided to do a Master's and began research for a thesis on Peadar O'Donnell – the renowned Irish republican and Marxist. Her initial interest in O'Donnell was political: in the late 1960s and early 1970s, he was one of the great figures of left-wing politics in Ireland, and he was also a prolific writer. However, she abandoned her thesis because she changed her mind about O'Donnell while she was carrying out her research. It wasn't that she became disillusioned with him, but more that she had a certain take on O'Donnell; by the time she got to the point of writing up her thesis, her view had changed – and she would have had to begin the research again. By that stage, her life had moved on, and the motivation to finish the thesis wasn't there. What marked her out was her intellectual openness: she was prepared to change her view on O'Donnell, despite all the work that she had invested in her research on him.

After university, I moved to Dublin. I had been elected president of the USI (the Union of Students in Ireland), and shared a rented house on Lindsay Road in Glasnevin. Around that time, Triona got a job in the Higher Education Authority. I remember that she came and stayed with us while she was doing the interviews. When she got the job, we had a vacant room in the house, so she came to live with us there, and later in Clontarf.

By then, I had got a job as an official in the Transport Union (then the ITGWU, now SIPTU, but always known to the people who worked in it as 'the Transport Union'). I worked first in Liberty Hall, then in Galway, and later in Kerry, where I was based in Tralee; I commuted back and forth to Dublin, as Carol was teaching in Bray. In 1979, when we bought a house, Triona moved in with us, which helped with the costs.

Carol and I married in 1981. It was a small wedding. We chose the beautiful Creeragh church in north Connemara for the ceremony, which was performed by Bishop Joe Cassidy. Afterwards, we all adjourned to the nearby Kylemore Pass Hotel; including Triona, the best man, Peter McEvoy, a friend from USI days, and the brides-maid, Rose Devlin, a childhood friend of Carol's from Killimor. Shortly after our wedding, I moved back to Dublin to start a new job in Liberty Hall, the headquarters of the ITGWU. Triona continued to live with us, and effectively became part of our family.

Carol and I had three children: Gráinne, Oisín and Seán. Being present at their births was the most wonderful experience of my life. I have just one brother, John, who lives in the United States, and Carol is an only child, so the children had no uncles and aunts in Ireland. Triona became Auntie Triona.

When Triona eventually moved out, she continued to fulfil her role as auntie to an extended brood. She never missed a birthday, and usually called in person to deliver the present and share the cake. Her visits were not confined to birthdays, though. She was a regular caller – usually around dinnertime. Grocery shopping on a Saturday always involved us making a judgement call about whether Triona was likely to visit, and how much food we needed to buy. I loved those Saturday evenings, as we cooked food, a glass of wine in one hand, the kitchen filled with conversation and laughter.

Intellectually, Triona was very powerful. She was actively involved in the women's movement. She had a strong theoretical grasp of politics and political philosophy, and of a vast range of subjects. I might start a conversation with her about some current issue, but she would take it to a different plane, examining it from a historical, or a philosophical perspective. She would talk about what she had just read and would often recommend books to me or lend them to me – knowing, I'm sure, that she was unlikely to get all of them back! She became a kind of intellectual soulmate of mine.

We shared the same political outlook, and she influenced me in many ways – some of which I came to appreciate only later. First of all, she was a very good friend, and friends always influence you, helping shape the way you do things. She also had a very calming influence on me: she was passionate about political issues, but I can't remember her ever raising her voice; we never fell out.

She was fundamentally open, and was always learning. She taught me that we all learn every day, and that it is vital to adjust our thinking based on the facts, on new evidence, and on our own experiences. We are all engaged in a lifelong learning process. That is how I approach politics. I have my principles, my basic beliefs, but I'm open as to how best to achieve certain ends. It really is a question of what works.

Take, for example, the way the social-welfare system works in Ireland – or, to be more precise, the way in which it is *not* working. The system, as I encounter it as a constituency TD, is trapping generations of people in poverty and maintaining them in a state of dependence. I believe strongly that people can be freed from poverty, but only if we are open to developing a system which is quite different from the kind of post-war welfare-state formula that we've been wedded to for the past fifty or sixty years. What we need is a system that enables people to achieve their potential and encourages them to progress. The social-welfare system should be centred on the idea of helping people lead a productive life rather than a dependent one, and should be much more closely linked to education and training, and encouraging people to return to work, than it is at the moment. We need to build not just a safety net, but a trampoline as well.

We have to balance political principles – the philosophical starting point of our thinking – with practicalities. As a social democrat, I see the world in a particular way, and I'm not about to change that. However, I *am* open to changing the way we achieve our aims in a particular area. The distinction between core principles and the practicalities of policy is widely accepted in many social-democratic parties across Europe. It was a key component of the book *The Future of Socialism*, by Anthony Crosland, which was published in 1956 and influenced a generation of Labour politicians in the UK.

Triona had that foundation: her basic beliefs were rock-solid, but she kept an open mind about how things might be done. We have to be open to changing our minds based on new evidence, or new thinking, without compromising our principles.

Healthcare is a good example of this. For many years, Labour people in Ireland looked to the National Health Service in the UK as the model of healthcare that we should seek to replicate here, because it seemed to offer a fairer and more accessible system. The NHS, however, was a creature of a particular moment in British history. It was set up immediately after the Second World War, at a time when medicine was far less high-tech than it is now. The world today is very different. About ten years ago, Liz McManus led a major re-examination of the Labour Party's health policy, and put forward the idea of universal health insurance. This system, which is used in other European countries, is based on the idea that healthcare is provided not through a large state bureaucracy but through an insurance system that ensures that 'money follows the patient'. The goals of the policy are the same as they always were – excellence, fairness and value for money – but the means of achieving them have changed. At the time, Labour's proposal was a pioneering one for Ireland, but in the intervening years more and more people and groups who want Ireland to have a better health service have become convinced that this is the route to take. Fianna Fáil attacked us, claiming that the system would be too bureaucratic, and set up the HSE instead!

We also have to base our thinking on our experience of real life – of how the issues that are debated in the Dáil and on the airwaves actually affect people in their day-to-day lives. Take the example of crime. As a constituency TD, I see the misery that low-level, so-called 'petty' crime can cause to decent citizens trying to go about their lives. Of course, I also see how crime often has its roots in poverty, or poor housing, or bad planning. But what explains crime can never excuse it, and I have little patience for those who dismiss anti-social behaviour as being somehow the fault of society. That being said, there is something very wrong about a system where a teacher can stand in front of a class of eight-year-olds and predict, with some accuracy, which of them are likely to end up with a prison record.

Triona led a hugely varied life. She reached a senior position in the HEA. I don't remember her ever discussing her work, though. That was part of her integrity. She was able to put up 'Chinese walls': to say 'That's my day job, and I'm not mixing that up with any other part of my life'. While she was Auntie Triona to us, her own family was a huge part of her life; she was always very close to her sister and brothers, and her mother and father. She lived life, and had a lot of time for her family and friends.

Triona died of cancer in June 2001. She was just forty-nine years old. She went for some tests and got some very bad news. For a time, she seemed to have overcome the illness, and then it came back. In the end I think she had two relapses. Her death was a massive loss to everyone who was close to her.

Carol and I miss her. I miss being able to discuss the issues of the day with her – to get her unique, cerebral take on the world. She is the kind of person who would provide a balanced view of our current situation. I wonder what her response would be to the economic crisis, and the impact it is having on our society. I also miss her company. She was such a warm person, with a wicked, spontaneous sense of humour. And nobody makes mulled wine like she used to make it.

4

Martin Luther King, Jr.

Violence as a way of achieving racial justice is both impractical and immoral. I am not unmindful of the fact that violence often brings about momentary results. Nations have frequently won their independence in battle. But in spite of temporary victories, violence never brings permanent peace. It solves no social problem: it merely creates new and more complicated ones. Violence is impractical because it is a descending spiral ending in destruction for all. It is immoral because it seeks to humiliate the opponent rather than win his understanding: it seeks to annihilate rather than convert. Violence is immoral because it thrives on hatred rather than love. It destroys community and makes brotherhood impossible. It leaves society in monologue rather than dialogue. Violence ends up defeating itself. It creates bitterness in the survivors and brutality in the destroyers.

Extract from Martin Luther King, Jr.'s acceptance speech, on being awarded the Nobel Peace Prize in Oslo, on 10 December 1964

In August 2008, I was invited to attend the Democratic National Convention in Denver, Colorado, where Barack Obama formally accepted the Democratic nomination for the presidency. While I was there, I took the opportunity to travel around the United States, including a visit to Memphis, Tennessee. Memphis has three shrines: its famous blues bars; Graceland, where Elvis Presley lived; and the Lorraine Motel, where Martin Luther King, Jr. was assassinated on 4 April 1968. Graceland certainly had the feel of a shrine. In fact, it reminded me of Knock: walking around it is a bit like going around the Stations of the Cross. Pilgrims move in hushed tones from one room to the next, ending up at Elvis's burial place, in the grounds of his former mansion. The Lorraine Motel was an entirely different experience.

King had come to Memphis twice in the month prior to his assassination, to show solidarity with the 1,300 African-American sanitation workers who had been on strike since February. The strike was provoked by an incident at the end of January, when severe weather prompted the civil authorities to send the black sanitation workers home without pay, while retaining the white workers. On 28 March 1968, King led a march of these workers through Memphis. Unfortunately, some incidents of violence and looting occurred, and they quickly spread. The police used tear gas, and the situation escalated, to a point where one protester was shot and killed.

King was appalled by the violence, which ran counter to everything on which his ideology of protest was founded. He decided to schedule another march for 8 April – as an example of how to conduct a non-violent protest. He arrived in Memphis on 3 April – later than planned, because of a bomb scare on the plane in which he was travelling. That evening, King made his now-famous 'I've been to the mountaintop' speech in the Mason Temple in Memphis. In the speech, he almost foretold his own early death:

> Like anybody, I would like to live a long life. Longevity has its place. But I'm not concerned about that now. I just want to do God's will. And he's allowed me to go up to the mountain. And I've looked over. And I've seen the Promised Land. I may not get there with you. But I want you to know tonight that we, as a people, will get to the Promised Land!

The Lorraine Motel, a two-storey building with balconies going all the way around, is a 1960s-style motel like the ones that feature in so many American movies from that decade. It is now a museum. It has been preserved as it was on the day of the assassination; I felt that it had an eerie feel. The tour walks visitors through what happened that day, from the time King and his group checked in. Some of them were standing out on the balcony when King was killed; the shot was fired from a boarding house across the road. I visited the boarding house, and stood at the window from which the sniper, James Earl Ray, fired the fatal shot. I found it very grisly, and somewhat voyeuristic. On the side of the road where the boarding house stands is a museum devoted to theories about the assassination. It is still unclear who might have been involved in it, and whether Ray acted alone: the King family came to believe that he did not.

The museum in the motel itself outlines King's life, and the growth of the civil rights movement. It also illustrates the fact that in the last years of his life, King and the other civil rights leaders, having achieved the right to vote for African-Americans, and the end of segregation, had started to fight for workers' rights. King had been supporting strikes by street cleaners and other municipal workers. As head of the FBI, J. Edgar Hoover suspected that social movements such as trade unions and civil rights organisations were vehicles for Communists, and first authorised the surveillance of Martin Luther King, Jr. for this reason in 1958. King always claimed that such allegations were used to smear the civil rights movement and obscure the real issue: racist segregation. However, he also observed that 'the Negro revolution is a genuine revolution, born from the same womb that produces all massive social upheavals – the womb of intolerable conditions and unendurable situations'.

I found the visit to be a very moving experience: King was only thirty-nine when he died. His life brings into sharp focus the clash between violence and non-violence: there is great irony in the fact that this man of peace, a passionate advocate of non-violence, was killed by a sniper's bullet.

Martin Luther King, Jr.'s involvement in the civil rights movement grew from his work as a churchman in Montgomery, Alabama, where he had been made a pastor in 1954, at just twenty-five years of age. When Rosa Parks refused to sit in the segregated part of a bus in Montgomery on 1 December 1955, King led the subsequent Montgomery bus boycott, which lasted 385 days. King's own house was bombed during the boycott. Over time, he became the acknowledged national leader of the movement – although some of the other leaders of the civil rights movement disagreed with the decision to take an exclusively non-violent approach.

King is an inspirational figure for the members of the many groups that developed from the civil rights movement, including the protests that led to the fall of communism. The American civil rights movement led to a whole wave of popular movements and forms of protest that were dignified, peaceful, powerful, and ultimately transformative – not least in the United States itself. In 1960, after winning the gold medal at the Rome Olympics, Muhammad Ali was famously told at a 'whites only' diner in Ohio: 'We don't serve niggers here.' His response? 'Well, I don't eat them either.' Five decades later, segregation, state-sanctioned racial discrimination, lynching, and the disenfranchisement of black people have been rendered embarrassing relics of the past, culminating in the election of Barack Obama as the first African-American president of the United States.

The background music of the 1960s and early 1970s, and to my own politicisation in university, was the music of protest, of non-violent political activity, and the demand by people for political and civil rights. In Ireland, we had the civil rights movement in the North, and more localised versions elsewhere. Gluaiseacht Chearta Sibhialta na Gaeltachta, for instance, was a campaign which began in Connemara to demand rights for Irish-language speakers in the Gaeltacht areas. There was a sense in the Gaeltacht that people who spoke Irish were regarded as second-class citizens. The leaders of the campaign wanted a greater recognition of the language, and the people who spoke it, but most of all, they wanted jobs. Grants and lip service would not keep the language alive, but employment opportunities and industrial development in Gaeltacht areas would. Ultimately, they achieved many of their objectives: the foundation of Údarás na Gaeltachta; a radio service, Raidió na Gaeltachta; and later TG4, set up by Labour's Michael D. Higgins. Then, much later, came the legislation recognising Irish as one of the languages of the European Union. I imagine that Martin Luther King, Jr. had no idea that his view from the mountaintop would stretch all the way to An Ceathrú Rua!

The civil rights movement in Northern Ireland was greatly influenced by the American civil rights movement, even down to the name they adopted: the Northern Ireland Civil Rights Association. The themes and the language used, and the issues which were taken up, were also very similar to those in America: voting rights, housing rights, access to employment, ways of dealing with a state where there is a supremacist majority, and where the police service and the courts abuse the minority. Even the anthem was the same: 'We shall overcome'.

The great success of the American civil rights movement was that it was a non-violent movement which succeeded in its aims. For me, it was this commitment to non-violence – embodied by Martin

Luther King, Jr. – that was, and still is, hugely inspirational and influential. King, and the movement he inspired, demonstrated that people could achieve their goals without using violence, even when they were threatened with, or subjected to, violence by their enemies. The great tragedy of the Northern Ireland civil rights movement was that it was sidelined by the sectarian campaigns of the paramilitary organisations, which evolved into a thirty-year campaign of violence, costing more than 3,500 lives and destroying the lives of many more.

King's civil rights movement was as vulnerable as any other to those on the fringes who were impatient to achieve their ends by any means, including violence. When a march, or a demonstration, is attacked by police or by a hostile opposition – as happened in Selma, Alabama, in 1965, for example, or Burntollet Bridge near Derry in 1969 – it is all too easy for these voices to become louder and more compelling. Yet it can be these very voices from within the organisation – not the clubs and bullets of the opposition – that can pose the greatest threat to the aims of a peaceful movement.

I abhor violence and am always inspired by those leaders, and those ordinary men and women, who are able to achieve their aims without it. Consider the death, destruction and bitterness – sometimes lasting generations – that has accompanied so much violent political change, including our own Civil War in the 1920s. Then consider how much Gandhi and Martin Luther King, Jr. achieved on the basis of peaceful mobilisation and political activity. They had to deal with the reaction of very powerful forces, but they operated on the basis that it is not he who inflicts the most, but he who can endure the most, who succeeds in the end. When I look back at the history of Northern Ireland, it is those who had the courage and humility to change whom I admire most – people like Terence O'Neill and David Trimble, who were ultimately defeated by the more intractable elements within Unionism. Indeed, sometimes it is those who give up power, not those who are seeking it, who demonstrate the most courage, because they have the most to lose from the changes that they help bring about.

So change was coming to Derry and Detroit in the 1960s and 1970s, but it was also coming in the Republic. T. K. Whitaker's reforms were bearing fruit, with new jobs being created on an unprecedented scale. The IDA was bringing in foreign direct investment, and for the first time since independence, most people had the opportunity to make a living in their own country. The introduction of free second-level education in 1967, followed by the new higher-education grants scheme in 1968, and the building of the regional technical colleges (now the Institutes of Technology), had laid the foundations for a revolution in education. When taken together, they gave an entire generation a real opportunity to go on to third-level education. I was one of many Irish people of that generation who were the first member of their family to go to college. This increase in participation in education inevitably raised people's expectations of what life in Ireland could, indeed should, offer them.

Increased levels of television ownership opened a window onto the rest of the world. In 1973, Ireland joined the European Community. For the first time since independence, we were beginning to think of ourselves not just as a former British colony, but as a European state on an equal footing with our neighbours. With the economy growing and incomes rising, people were travelling more too. It was an exciting time to be on the cusp of adulthood.

I became active in student politics in the 1970s, when I went to UCG. I had started college in 1972, four years after Martin Luther King, Jr. was assassinated. The same year, there was a successful referendum to reduce the voting age to eighteen. However, Jack Lynch called the election in 1973 – a month before the new electoral register came into effect. Therefore, even though those of us under the age of twenty-one had won the right to vote, we couldn't exercise it. (In fact, I wouldn't have been able to vote anyway, because I wasn't eighteen until later that year.) I suspect that Lynch called the election to disenfranchise that cohort of young people who had won the vote in the previous referendum. As a result, the bulk of students didn't get the opportunity to vote until the following general election, in 1977. These days, an eighteen-year-old can vote – and thus has some influence on their local politicians. Before 1972 – in fact, right up to the 1977 general election – if you were under twenty-one, you were politically invisible. For younger people, this made protest activity all the more important.

The non-violent protests of the southern states of America provided a blueprint for the student movement across Europe. Here in Ireland, it no doubt influenced the big student demonstrations which were organised in the late sixties and seventies about student grants and the need for education reform. I was a part of that movement. In 1974, I was elected President of the UCG Student Union, and went on to be elected twice as President of the Union of Students of Ireland (USI) from 1976 to 1978.

Over that time, we succeeded in getting substantial increases in student grants, in the introduction of degree-level courses in the teacher education colleges and the colleges of technology, and we developed a range of student union and student welfare services. But I think our biggest achievement was in maintaining a united student movement in Northern Ireland throughout a very sectarian and violent period of the troubles.

As in many other walks of life in Northern Ireland, students from a Catholic or Nationalist background looked to Dublin and the USI as their national union, while students from a Protestant or Unionist background looked to the National Union of Students in the UK (NUSUK). In the USI, we worked with the NUSUK within a structure whereby students in Northern Ireland were members of both national unions simultaneously, and we did not allow them to choose between the two. That kept the student body united and helped to keep sectarianism out of student union politics. One of those with whom I worked closely on this was my counterpart, President of the NUSUK Charles Clarke, who went on to become Home Secretary in Tony Blair's government.

It was in this political ferment in the mid-seventies that I joined a political party. My family's political loyalties were with Fianna Fáil.

Indeed, the very first vote I ever cast was, at my mother's request, for a Fianna Fáil candidate in the 1974 local elections. However, I felt Fianna Fáil was a deeply conservative party, particularly on social issues.

In UCG, I became involved with the left-leaning student discussion group called the Movement for Social Progress. I subsequently campaigned for the Labour Party and Michael D. Higgins in the 1973 general election.

In 1975, at the age of twenty, and towards the end of my term of office as President of the Student Union, I joined the UCG Republican Club, which was affiliated to Official Sinn Féin, later re-named the Workers' Party. I felt that they were the most vigorous in campaigning for a modern Ireland and for real social change. I also felt that they were the most courageous in standing up to the sectarian violence that was being conducted by the Provos in Northern Ireland, and supported by Provisional Sinn Féin.

Change was in the air, and the American civil rights movement, with Martin Luther King, Jr. as its leader, had a phenomenal, indirect influence on the movements that were under way to modernise Ireland. Those campaigns achieved far greater levels of equality than had been possible before, challenged authority and the status quo, and played a huge part in changing the country in numerous fundamental ways.

I believe that, of all these campaigns, the women's movement had the greatest impact on Irish society. When I entered university, my female contemporaries were expected to work at the same job as a man, in teaching or other professions, for salaries that were around a third less than those of their male counterparts. The marriage bar, which required women to retire from jobs in the public service when they married, was only abolished in 1973. In a job interview, a woman could be asked about everything from who was going to mind the children, to who would make her husband's dinner if she got the job! The establishment of an unconditional right to economic independence was one of the most important leaps forward for Irish women: it allowed them not only to control their own career and their income, but also to decide when, or whether, they would marry.

However, it was the agenda of personal freedom – of contraception, of fertility, of sexual freedom – which brought not just women, but also Irish society as a whole, into direct conflict with the authority of the Catholic Church. More than anything else, it was this challenge to the power which had been exercised by the church over Irish society for so long that was to bring about the most far-reaching changes. Significantly, the pressure for change came from the bottom up. One thing was abundantly clear: conservative politicians, who had allowed the Catholic Church to have an unofficial seat at the Cabinet table from the earliest days of independence, could not be counted on to initiate reform. It would have to come from elsewhere – and it did. The modernisation of Ireland became the cause of a generation of activists and campaigners; the foundations were laid for legislative reform that would, for the most part, be enacted by the Labour Party in government.

From the vantage point of today's Ireland, it can be hard to comprehend just how difficult that struggle was. While the women's movement in Ireland mirrored similar efforts to attain equal rights for women elsewhere, the dominance of Catholic social teaching in Irish society and politics, and even in our Constitution, meant that women's attempts to assert control over their own sexuality was to draw the church, the state, and its citizens into a conflict that went to the heart of what it meant to live in a modern democracy. At the core of this conflict was the struggle for the right to a private life, where matters of sexual morality were decided by an individual, not the state.

This battle was about issues that were very personal, and sometimes very intimate; they were played out in public in a way that people simply would not stand for today. A seminal moment was the 1973 case of Mary McGee, a married mother of four who successfully argued, all the way to the Supreme Court, that the ban on contraceptives was a contravention of marital privacy. The McGee case, which was championed by Mary Robinson, established the right of married couples to import contraceptives for their own use, but it was not until the Health (Family Planning) Act of 1979 – famously introduced by Minister for Health Charles J. Haughey as an 'Irish solution to an Irish problem' – that it became legal to purchase contraception in Ireland, though only on prescription from a doctor! It was not until 1985 that Labour TD Barry Desmond, then Minister for Health in the Labour-Fine Gael coalition government, made it legal for over-eighteens to buy condoms without a prescription. The sale of condoms was finally deregulated as late as 1992 – by another Labour minister, Brendan Howlin.

This three-decade-long challenge to the authority of the Catholic Church sparked off other liberalising reforms that gradually took the state out of citizens' bedrooms, and the Catholic Church out of areas where it had previously exercised a monopoly. Industrial schools for poor children, and Magdalene laundries for unmarried mothers, closed their doors. Fewer tragic stories of unmarried mothers and dead babies surfaced in the newspapers. Homosexuality was decriminalised in 1993, again at the behest of Labour in government. A referendum to permit separated people to divorce and remarry was finally carried – by a margin of only nine thousand votes – in 1995. I was, by then, a member of the government committee which organised the divorce referendum. In 1997, the Dáil passed some of the most progressive equal-rights legislation in Europe – legislation which had been drafted by the Labour Minister for Equality and Law Reform, Mervyn Taylor.

Ireland today is a more equal, more tolerant place than it was when I started university in the early 1970s, precisely because a critical mass of people fought to make it so – often in the face of vociferous opposition. Younger people I meet often say that their generation has no cause left to fight for – that the big struggles for equality and freedom have been won. I cannot agree. Ireland still has some way to travel before we can say that ours is a truly equal society, where each citizen has the freedom to reach their full potential, regardless of their background.

*

The civil rights movement went to the heart of how we regard our fellow human beings. It challenged people to decide whether they were for equal treatment of every person, simply by virtue of their humanity – or not.

Most notions of a fair society involve some form of equality. Yet while most people would agree with the idea of equality, the critical question is: equality of what?

Take Mary Harney's formulation of what her former party, the Progressive Democrats, believe constitutes equality (quoted in the 26 July 2004 *Irish Times*):

> Equality of opportunity is central to our [the PDs'] political belief. It does not mean we abdicate our responsibilities to those on the margins, or leave them to fend for themselves. There will always be those who will need ongoing support, and it is our duty to care for those who cannot care for themselves. But people who can help themselves should have the opportunity for improvement and advancement, and they should be rewarded on the basis of what they have achieved. This principle is an integral part of what I would call a fair society.

Here, the answer to the question 'Equality of what?' is 'Equal opportunity to amass wealth'. For neo-liberal politicians like Mary Harney, taxation and state regulation should not be allowed to get in the way of the right of individuals to increase their income and to accumulate assets. She is careful to point out that she would like to maintain a welfare state that deals with 'basic inequality' – those who 'cannot care for themselves' – but it is up to everyone else to ride 'equal opportunity' into the sunset of self-sufficiency.

I agree with Mary Harney in one respect: people who work hard deserve to be rewarded for their efforts, and people should have an equal opportunity to do this. Where we differ is in how we believe equality of opportunity can be achieved. Neo-liberal philosophy – the kind that has dominated Irish politics and economic policy since 1997 – believes that equality of opportunity is achieved by having the state step back, ensuring that there are basic health and education services for those who will never be able to afford to 'go private', and letting people get on with the business of working and making money. However, this is an extremely simplistic view of equality of opportunity – one which might make sense in a textbook but which has no bearing on how the world actually works.

It is of little comfort to know that we are all theoretically equal in terms of our right to work hard and accumulate wealth, if many of our citizens lack the basic requirements to avail of that freedom. Simply standing back and allowing people to develop themselves unhindered is not enough. The state – that is us, as a community – also has a positive role to play, to provide people with the means to develop their abilities themselves, and to help them to do so.

Real equality demands more than the negative freedom from state interference; it demands a reasonable measure of equality of resources. There is little point in providing free education for all, if a child goes to school too hungry to concentrate on her lessons.

There is no point in saying that women have equal rights in the workplace, unless you match that with decent provisions for paid maternity leave. There is no real equality of opportunity for an elderly person who needs a hip operation, without which they have difficulty moving, if they have to wait years for their operation. Equality does not mean sameness, whether sameness of income or ability – though some choose to caricature it as such. Rather, equality comes from empowering people to develop their own gifts and abilities, to work hard, and to make a contribution to society.

It is the building of this kind of society which is the greatest challenge for this generation. Central to that challenge is organising our state, and our society, so that it is judged not simply by how people are protected from life's hardships, but by the reach and the quality of their opportunities. There is no 'equality' in poverty traps, nor in a social-welfare system that does not reward responsibility. Equality is not something that is bestowed by the fortunate on the less well-off, though any progressive tax system would adhere to the maxim 'from each according to his ability, to each according to his needs'. Rather, an equal society is a collective endeavour, which each of us has a responsibility to help create through our actions.

While this agenda could broadly be described as achieving equality through developing people's capabilities – an idea popularised by Nobel Prize-winning economist Amartya Sen – there are still some battles to be won in the fight for equal citizenship. One example is the right of gay couples in committed relationships to marry each other. It is a sign of how much Ireland has changed that a recent Bill giving gay couples the right to a civil union, with similar rights to those of married people, was passed by all-party consensus in the Dáil without the need for a vote. Of course, civil union is not the same as marriage for gay couples – a right to which I believe gay people, as citizens of our country, are entitled. The Labour Party was the first political party to publish far-reaching legislation on civil unions for same-sex couples in 2003; this legislation was intended as a stepping stone to full marriage equality, a right which would need to be decided by referendum.

Another area where we still have work to do is in relation to equality between men and women. As I discussed earlier, the women's movement in Ireland was successful in many of its objectives – so successful, indeed, that many young people no longer think that feminism is relevant to their lives. However, there are still many parts of Irish life where men and women do not have a level playing pitch. One of those is pay: men still earn an average of 13 percent more than women, on an hour-for-hour basis. Another area is politics: despite the fact that women make up just over 50 percent of the population, only 14 percent of TDs are women. The only place I have ever encountered a worse gender balance than the Dáil was in my all-boys boarding school! This situation does not reflect modern Irish life, or the modern workplace. The Labour Party does moderately well in this regard – one third of our TDs are women – but we could do better, which is why we plan to enact a law making public funding for political parties conditional on the relative number of women they put forward as candidates.

These are by no means the only examples of areas where we could improve the quality of Irish citizenship. Ireland, and Irish attitudes, have changed profoundly over the past few decades. We are coming to terms with living in a globalised society, where many traditional certainties – the respective roles of men and women, the role and status of the Catholic Church, the concept of a 'job for life' – have changed utterly. Today more than one in ten of our population was not born here. The party of de Valera and Lemass, of service to the Republic, became the party of dig-outs and golden circles. Never has the image of the past as a different country been so apt. Of course, many of our values have endured: the importance of family; the fact that more than 90 percent of the population still identify themselves as adhering to one religion or another; and perhaps a helathy scepticism when it comes to authority.

Yet despite all the change that has taken place, Ireland is still governed by a set of rules which were written in the 1930s, for the 1930s. The Constitution dates from a time when one church was considered to have a special position in society, and women were considered to be second-class citizens. It has served many adults well, but has failed too many children. I believe that it is time for a fundamental review of the Constitution. This would be an opportunity to reflect not only on the aspects of the Consitution that have served us well, but also on our aspirations for our country, and ourselves as citizens, in the twenty-first century. I have my own suggestions as to what might be included – a right to a second-level education, for example, or a right to shelter – but I am just one of the citizens to whom the Constitution belongs, and at the end of the day, I only have one vote. I have proposed the establishment of a Constitutional Convention, made up of elected representatives, members of civil society, and ordinary citizens chosen at random – in the same way as they are for jury duty – which would be a forum for debate and the development of ideas for a new Constitution, one that reflects the values and the ideals of modern Ireland, and that would serve us for the decades to come. The new Constitution would be voted on by referendum, much like the 1937 version.

*

Martin Luther King, Jr. reminds us that, for such a simple concept, equality is revolutionary. It can topple governments and start wars. It asks that we treat others as we would be treated ourselves. The struggle for equality has modernised Ireland and made it a more compassionate, fairer place to live; by continuing that struggle, we can make it fairer still. But mostly, in the words of another civil rights hero, Robert F. Kennedy, in 1961, we will continue to fight for equality:

> not because it is economically advantageous – although it is; not because the laws of God and man command it – although they do command it; not because people in other lands wish it so. We must do it for the single and fundamental reason that it is the right thing to do.

5
Seán O'Casey

Whenever we think or talk about the role that Labour has played in Irish history, the iconic figures of James Connolly and Jim Larkin immediately spring to mind. These two giants of history represent for many of us the part that Labour played in securing Irish freedom, and in the struggle to improve conditions for working people. That will never change. When it comes to telling the Labour story, however, and thinking about the future role of Labour in Irish life, the figure I keep coming back to is Seán O'Casey.

Labour's emblem, the red rose, is always associated in my mind with O'Casey. The rose is widely used by socialist and social-democratic parties around the world. Its use as a symbol has several origins, including the struggle in the US for better working conditions for women factory workers. For the Labour Party in Ireland, however, the rose symbol is inspired by O'Casey's quotation about James Larkin, when he said that here was a leader 'who would put a flower in a vase on a table as well as a loaf on a plate'. The bread part is easy to understand: the Labour movement is clearly about material things, having its origin in the struggle to tackle poverty and to ensure that people have enough to eat and a roof over their head. So it's certainly about bread. But it's also about roses. It's about things of the soul and the spirit: cultural things. It's about education, the arts, music and the environment. Essentially, it's about quality of life. The rose emblem encapsulates that ideal, neatly summarised by that line of O'Casey's.

The first time I saw an O'Casey play, I was about eleven or twelve. It was around the time of the commemoration of the fiftieth anniversary of the 1916 Rising; I recall seeing *The Plough and the Stars* on television. This was around the same time that RTÉ did a series called *Insurrection*, about the rebellion and the occupation of the GPO. The series was action stuff, not dissimilar to the cowboy movies that were popular at the time; of course for me, as a young boy, the more shooting there was, the more I liked it! *Insurrection* presented Easter 1916 as an exciting, militaristic event; it was very much in the classical tradition of the way history was taught in Ireland. Here were the brave Irish fighting to get the Brits out of Ireland. There was a particular scene in *The Plough and the Stars* that was in the same vein. In many ways, to my young eyes, it was like *Insurrection*, with Jack Clitheroe, one of the main characters in the play, strutting around in his Citizen Army uniform.

However, the *The Plough and the Stars* presents the human side of that type of conflict, and the human suffering that results from it.

One of the most memorable, and most painful, scenes is the one in which Nora Clitheroe begs Jack Clitheroe not to go out to fight. That theme is present throughout O'Casey's plays: the questioning of the validity of the armed struggle.

This was a very personal issue for O'Casey. He was born John Casey (or perhaps John Cassidy), to a lower-middle-class Protestant family in Dublin; his father died when he was six years old, and the family's fortunes declined steadily thereafter. O'Casey's eyesight was poor, and he received only a few years of formal schooling. Growing up amidst the slums and tenements of Dublin, O'Casey was attracted first to the Gaelic revival, and then to socialism, becoming a significant figure in the labour movement. He was one of the founding members of the Citizen Army, which was formed in 1913 in response to the death and injury of striking workers on the streets of Dublin. He was the Citizen Army's secretary, though he later resigned from the organisation, and parted company entirely from the armed struggle.

What O'Casey does in his work – and the reason I'm interested in him – is that he takes us behind the political and military struggle, and into the homes of the people who lived through it. He enables us to see what was happening from the viewpoint of the people who experienced it. Like the Easter Rising, the 1913 Lockout is written about in heroic terms; the strike is spoken about, and sung about, as a great, heroic labour struggle. What we don't get from that presentation is the suffering – particularly the suffering of women and their families. This aspect, which was central to people's experience of the period, is often overlooked. O'Casey understands this, and humanises the whole period. He brings to life the people who were there, and he does so with great humour. O'Casey's plays present us with truly great characters; they are also great Dublin plays.

In the run-up to the centenary of the 1916 Rising, we should, as a country, rediscover O'Casey: his plays, his other writings, and his interpretation of armed conflict and the suffering it brings. While there will be enormous attention given to the centenary, it is only one of a series of anniversaries that are approaching, connected to what was one of the most significant periods of Irish history. In 2009, we had the centenary of the formation of the Irish Transport and General Workers' Union. (For those who are interested, Francis Devine has produced two fine histories of the ITGWU.) In 2012, the Labour Party will celebrate its centenary, and in 2013, of course, we will have the centenary of the Lockout. (Padraig Yeates' book *Lockout: Dublin, 1913* is an excellent account of that period.) We are also looking towards the centenaries of the formation of the Volunteers, the outbreak of the First World War, the general election of 1918, the meeting of the First Dáil in 1919, and then the whole period of the War of Independence, leading up to the signing of the Treaty in 1921.

These anniversaries provide an opportunity to correct a serious imbalance in the way that Irish history, as it has traditionally been taught and presented, has neglected and downplayed the role of the labour movement during the period from 1909 to 1922. To take but one example, the series of documentaries done by RTÉ, *Seven Ages*, simply wrote organised labour out of the history of this country. In fact, the labour movement made a vital contribution to the fight for independence, most obviously through the involvement of James Connolly and the Citizen Army in 1916, but also in a variety of other ways.

During the period between 1916 and the beginning of the War of Independence, Labour was a driving force in Irish politics at a time when Sinn Féin was still recovering from the fallout of the 1916 Rising. The labour movement was central to the campaign to stop the British government, which was increasingly desperate for troops, from extending conscription to Ireland in 1918. The unions organised a general strike, which was widely supported, and played a crucial role in uniting the country in opposition to conscription. There was also a ban on moving munitions. It was this unity of national purpose that laid the groundwork for the election of 1918. At the election itself, Labour, which stood to make substantial gains, withdrew its candidates, in order to avoiding splitting the independence vote. The result was the destruction of the Irish Parliamentary Party, and a landslide for Sinn Féin.

Following the 1918 election, Sinn Féin TDs refused to take their seats in Westminster, and established the first Dáil. At its first meeting, the Dáil adopted a number of documents, the most significant of which was the Democratic Programme; this document was largely written by the Labour Party leader, Tom Johnson. Johnson was a remarkable figure: although his role in our history is little remembered, he was a key player in many of the great events of this period. Indeed, in 1927, Johnson came within a single vote of becoming Taoiseach (or President of the Executive Council, as the position was then known). An agreement was made that Fianna Fáil would take their seats in the Dáil and support the Labour nominee for leadership of the government. The story goes that a Sligo deputy, Alderman Jinks, was taken off to Buswells to be entertained, and Johnson lost by one vote.

The Democratic Programme itself, though little remembered now, expresses the hopes and aspirations of the new nation at its foundation. Too much of the story of this time is expressed in simplistic terms as a struggle for independence – to get the Brits out. Far too little attention is paid to what those involved in the independence movement thought an independent Ireland could achieve. Nonetheless, there *was* an economic and social dimension to all of this – much of it provided by the Labour movement. It is believed, for example, that Connolly was responsible for the social elements in the 1916 proclamation, which offered 'equal rights and equal opportunities' to all its citizens. These ideas were then amplified and expanded, in elegant and sometimes stirring language, by Johnson, in the Democratic Programme. It is a document from which we can still draw inspiration, and which, indeed, reproaches us, such as when it proclaims that the first duty of the government of the Republic is to its children. How often our state has failed to live up to that goal.

As 2016 approaches, there is an opportunity to look again at the role of Labour in the tumultuous events of that period. There will, I hope, be a rediscovery of the writings of James Connolly, just as there was at the time of the fiftieth anniversary of 1916, when his works were republished. We will hear a lot too about Larkin and his contribution to the development of the labour movement in Ireland. We should also rediscover some of the less well-known figures, such as Tom Johnson and William O'Brien – who picked up the reins of the ITGWU after Connolly was shot and Larkin went to America, and who was also a leading figure in the Labour Party. (There is a fine biography of O'Brien by Father Thomas Morrissey.) The Irish Labour History Society has worked over many years to preserve this valuable part of our history. We now have an opportunity to write labour *back into* our history; Seán O'Casey should be a part of this.

There is an integrity and honesty in O'Casey's writing. It is thought-provoking even today; when it was written, it represented a direct challenge to the consensus of the time. When *The Plough and the Stars* was first staged at the Abbey, the audience rioted, provoking W. B. Yeats to walk up on to the stage and address the audience with his famous rebuke: 'You have disgraced yourselves once again.' (The 'again' apparently referred to the audience's reaction to *The Playboy of the Western World* in 1907.) In refusing to glorify violence, and in setting his play in the urban tenements and slums, whose occupants were hit hardest by the conflict – as is always the case – O'Casey was one of the few who captured the essence of those times in his writings.

Then, as now, O'Casey challenges the orthodox interpretation of the independence period. It is no coincidence that O'Casey, along with the activities of the labour movement, has been somewhat side-lined in conventional Irish history: he questioned events, and didn't go along with the received wisdom, which has largely prevailed. This is the courage that defines good art and good literature: the creative work that stands the test of time. Seán O'Casey absolutely refused to glorify violence. He simply faced that view down, and made pow-erful statements on the subject. He was asking the audience to look again at the meaning of violence and armed conflict, and the conse-quences of them.

Just as O'Casey discomfited his audiences in the 1920s, he will pose difficult questions for us as we approach 2016. There is no doubting that 1916 was a pivotal moment in Irish history, or that the rebellion was central to the birth of the independent Ireland of which we are rightly proud. But we will also have to confront our tendency to glorify the violence and conflict that is such a signifi-cant part of our history. O'Casey is so important because he coun-terbalances that impulse.

Part of what makes O'Casey so relevant is that he was there. He was part of the leadership of the Citizen Army. O'Casey believed in the use of force in self-defence, but he then lived through it, and eventually came to a point where he reconsidered his position. He began to question the move towards armed conflict, and ultimately rejected this approach. His role as witness as well as writer has absolute validity here. I have often thought of the Troubles in

Northern Ireland in this context: I believe that O'Casey would have rejected the armed struggle, on the grounds of the suffering it inflicted, and also because of what it did to deepen sectarian divisions among the people.

We have glorified 1916 and the War of Independence, and we have buried the Civil War. Now, I think there are signs of post hoc glorification of the Troubles, such as various recent documentaries which romanticise prison escapes and other aspects of that conflict. I certainly subscribe to the view that the war is over and that we have to let bygones be bygones; we have to heal wounds and move on from the conflict. But I also think it's a mistake to romanticise past conflicts and to fail to evaluate them critically in terms of the suffering they caused. This is why I would argue for the rediscovery of O'Casey. When we come to look at what happened in that period – as we will, over the next few years – O'Casey has to be part of the narrative.

O'Casey's writing had another outstanding quality. He had an intuitive understanding of people, along with an identification with them and their everyday lives and concerns. I think he understood hunger. He understood what it's like to be in a home with children that you can't feed, because you have no money to buy food. I think he understood the domestic tensions which poverty produces. He understood the conflict between a mother, whose first priority is to put food on the table for her children and make sure there is a fire in the grate, and a husband, who has a different peer group, perhaps in the trade union or in the pub or somewhere else, which drives him to be on the picket line first thing in the morning. If you're in the pub, or in the union hall, or on the picket line, you have the advantage of not seeing hungry children all the time.

For my own part, when I worked as a trade union official, I saw it as my job to negotiate with the employer to try to solve disputes – to use the industrial-relations machinery to find some way of achieving resolution, and avoiding a strike. I always regarded a strike as a failure, as something that people endure; there are no winners in a strike.

O'Casey presents a challenge, not just to how we think about the independence movement, but also to how the labour movement understands its own history. I am not in any way diminishing the heroism of people who went on strike to fight for, and assert, their rights. At the same time, accounts of labour history tend to focus on the heroic or dramatic events. We see the conflict between the employer and the employee. We see the injustices in the workplace, the people who were sacked, the people who had to turn up to the hiring fairs in the morning and wait to be hired on a casual basis. We see the injustice of low pay, and the exploitation of workers. And we see the decision to join a trade union and make the very courageous decision to go on strike, and to experience the uncertainty of whether you will ever get your job back – and, of course, the loss of income that goes with being on strike. This is one part of the labour heritage, not just here but elsewhere. And then there have been critical moments, such as the big, political strikes, like 1913 and 1918 in Ireland, and the general strike in Britain in 1926.

That is all part of a heroic narrative. In the case of Ireland, we also have the role of Connolly and the Citizen Army in the 1916 Rising. The great slogan 'We serve neither King nor Kaiser', emblazoned on a banner across Liberty Hall, which was itself bombarded by the Helga gunboat in 1916. Each year, the Labour Party organises a commemoration at Arbour Hill, where we pay tribute to Connolly; I am proud to address the commemoration as leader of the Labour Party. For all of us in the Labour Party, James Connolly is the founder of our party and of our movement. He is a huge, iconic figure. But all of that, important as it is, is only one part of the story.

The importance of O'Casey is that he writes the human narrative. He gets behind the banners, the flags, the marching bands and the picket lines, and tells us about what's happening in homes, in the stairwells. He also communicates these situations, and describes them in language which people would have used every day. We have the speeches of Connolly and Larkin for ever more – their writings, their proclamations and their declarations. These are the political, public description and story, but for an understanding of the everyday experience, of the poverty which was always there along with the struggle, we have far fewer records to which we can turn. What makes O'Casey unique is that he has written from inside the tenement. What he has given us is invaluable.

O'Casey's portrayal of Ireland and the Irish at that time did not sit easily with the official version of a newly free and independent nation. Ireland was a poor country at the time of independence, and remained so for many decades afterwards, right up until the 1960s. It took a very long time to get rid of the appalling, nineteenth-century-type poverty in this country, to improve housing and to get rid of the tenements.

Even today, we still have the modern versions of the stairwells that were the setting for O'Casey's plays. There are disadvantaged areas and communities that have problems with drugs, with educational disadvantage, with inter-generational poverty and dependence. Like Johnson's Democratic Programme, O'Casey's plays remind us of what is still unfinished. We have not conquered poverty, or eradicated illiteracy.

O'Casey stands, therefore, as a reminder to the labour movement that the aspirations of Connolly and Larkin have not yet been fulfilled, and that freedom for our country must also mean freedom for our people – in terms of freedom from poverty, and the freedom that comes with education. It is a reminder of the importance of providing good housing. His plays are a rebuke from the past, reminding us of what we should be looking to achieve in the future.

I find it interesting that, over the course of time, the emblem of the Irish Labour Party moved from being the Starry Plough of Connolly and the Citizen Army, and became the rose. We are, and always will be, Connolly's party, but I don't think we acknowledge sufficiently the significance of our connection with Seán O'Casey and *his* red rose.

This re-examination of the role of Labour in Ireland's past is important, particularly as the Labour Party is offering itself as potentially the leading component of an Irish government, based on the issues of the day and the things that concern people now. In doing this, we have to be mindful of where the labour movement has come from, and we need to understand that the history of the labour movement is also an untold part of our national history, as it has been written and presented up to now. No other party, and no other movement, captures the strands that make up modern Ireland as well as the labour movement does.

Up to now, the history of the labour movement has largely been presented as a history of trade unions and industrial conflict: the role of the Citizen Army in the Rising and the early years, and then, later, the role played by the Labour Party in different stages of Ireland's national development. But this is far too limiting. We have to look at the labour movement today as drawing not just on the trade union tradition and on the history of industrial conflict and struggles in the workplace, but on a much wider and more complex history.

Ours is the history of the women's movement; the campaign for personal freedoms; the peace movement; the demand for artistic and cultural freedom. It is both an urban phenomenon and a rural one. It is the story not just of Jack Clitheroe, but also of his wife Nora. It is the story of one Ireland.

6
Joan Miley

After I finished my term as president of USI in 1978, I went to work for the Irish Transport and General Workers' Union. I was one of a group of nine union officials who were recruited at that time, in what was a major departure from the union's normal recruitment practice. Traditionally, union officials were employed on a one-by-one basis; very often, they were volunteer activists or shop stewards in their own workplace who then became officials in that branch of the union. In the late 1970s, however, the union decided to recruit a body of trainee officials who would learn about and become familiar with all aspects of the job from the outset. The idea was that we would do courses in subjects such as labour law, negotiating skills and economics; the union hadn't taken such an organised approach to these things before. Since many of these new recruits were third-level graduates, one wag declared 'they are destroying the union by degrees'!

I worked for the union from 1978 until my election to the Dáil in 1989. Today, that might seem like an unusual career path – staying for so long in what was effectively my first job after college. In fact, it was an immensely varied role, and gave me a practical insight into a large swath of the commercial and economic life of the country. I had the privilege of representing people from all over Ireland and all walks of life. In many ways, it served as an excellent training ground for my later work in politics. It also brought me into contact with some extraordinary people, including Joan Miley.

I spent the first few months in my new job in the union's head office in Liberty Hall doing a variety of things, just like any rookie. Then the branch secretary in Galway had to go out on sick leave around Christmas of 1978; because I was from Galway, I was asked to go there to deputise for him. So it happened that, relatively soon after I began working for the Transport Union, I was an acting branch secretary. It was very much a case of being thrown in at the deep end!

One dispute I particularly remember concerned refuse trucks. This dispute went to the Labour Court, and thereafter to a ballot for strike action. Our timing, as it happened, was a bit unfortunate: the strike was planned to start about two weeks before the Pope was due to visit Galway. No effort was spared in finding a way of settling the strike before he arrived. While this worked to the advantage of the members, the union was concerned that its actions might be misinterpreted. The day before the Pope arrived, a papal flag was dispatched to me from Liberty Hall; I was ordered to hang it out the window of the union office, and was warned that a check would be made to ensure that I had complied with the edict!

While in Galway, I was deeply involved in organising the tax marches of 1979 and 1980. PAYE workers felt that they were bearing a disproportionate share of the country's tax burden, and took their protest to the streets.

The first PAYE march was organised by the Dublin Council of Trade Unions, and soon the protest spread to other cities. The first tax march in Galway was organised by the ITGWU for a Sunday morning, and I was in the thick of it. Later, marches were organised by the Galway Council of Trade Unions. The largest of these took place in early 1980, culminating in a rally in Eyre Square, at which I spoke. Descending from the platform at the end of the rally, I asked an ambulance driver for his estimate of the crowd. He took a moment to consider, before replying: 'This is as big as a Connacht final in Castlebar – there must be 20,000 here!' And there were.

Shortly after that, I received a phone call from the union's general secretary, Michael Mullen, offering to appoint me branch secretary in Tralee. At that time, Tralee was one of the biggest branches in the union, so it was no small offer. As it transpired, there had been a competition for branch secretary, and both the executive of the union and the branch committee in Tralee were divided on who should be appointed. The solution was to appoint somebody from outside. I would spend the best part of two years in Tralee, working in what was a big, mixed industrial branch. By autumn 1981, however, Carol and I were newly married, and she was working in Bray. She wasn't keen on moving to Kerry, so I applied for the job of secretary of the professional and managerial branch. Luckily, I was successful. By the end of 1981, I was back in Dublin working in a new position in Liberty Hall.

Although I was based in the capital, the job took me around the country, and to a wide range of workplaces. The membership of the branch mainly consisted of managerial-level employees, as well as some professional staff. We had a lot of public-sector managers, like county managers and regional tourism managers, and also some senior managers from the semi-state companies. Many of the members were people who had been trade union members and activists, very often shop stewards, and had been promoted to management in the private sector. It was frequently the practice of private companies – and still is, although to a far lesser extent – to recruit shop stewards as managers because they were individuals with proven leadership skills. This was the 1980s, and in many companies, employees would retain their union membership when they moved into managerial positions. We also recruited people who came to the union, very often on a purely confidential basis; these were often quite senior managers in multinational companies who did not want their company to know that they were members of the union. They were joining the union partly in order to provide themselves with some level of protection if anything went wrong, but mainly to seek advice of one kind or another. I did a lot of work advising managers about the levels of salaries that they should expect, as well as reward packages and pension schemes. Our members also included teachers in private fee-paying schools. The job was very varied, and I thoroughly enjoyed it.

Then, some time in 1984, I received a phone call from John Carroll, who was by then general president of the ITGWU, asking for a favour. The Irish Federation of Musicians and Allied Professions had been engaged in a long process of amalgamating with the ITGWU – one of several amalgamations that had taken place over the years. In the final stage of this merger, however, things started to unravel. As John Carroll described it, the ITGWU wanted to pull back from the amalgamation and let the two unions go their separate ways. The problem was that there was an outstanding pay claim for the musicians in both of the RTÉ orchestras – the National Symphony Orchestra and the Concert Orchestra – and this would have to be processed first.

All I was being asked to do, John told me, was to take the claim, get a settlement from RTÉ or bring it to the Labour Court, get it to a point where the musicians accepted either an offer from RTÉ or a Labour Court recommendation, and bring the matter to a conclusion. He made it clear that I wasn't being *told* to do this, but in reality I was being asked for a favour, and I felt I had to say yes. The first step was to meet with the section committee of the RTÉ orchestras, including its chairperson, Joan Miley.

From the beginning, I remember how forthright Joan was, but also how that directness was combined with a sharp intelligence and a sparkling sense of humour. Joan had been a violinist in the RTÉ NSO since it was formed in 1948; she was, in effect, the principal union representative of the musicians. The claim itself was of long-standing and somewhat complicated origin; it was clear from the beginning that this would not be an easy one. At one stage in that first meeting, I offered the opinion that perhaps we could negotiate on the basis of productivity. I remember Joan's response: 'Does this mean we will be expected to play faster?' We then started to go through the various working conditions of the musicians, and they explained to me how much they had to pay for musical instruments. I asked – rather naively, I suppose – why RTÉ didn't supply them with their musical instruments. Joan again gave a memorable reply: 'We are not like county council workers. We can't walk in each morning and pick up the next shovel we're offered! These are violins!' In fact, I remember that when we itemised the cost of their musical instruments, I was taken aback by the price of some of them. A new oboe came in at the princely sum of £1,500.

What followed was a long and tortuous process, as we conducted our negotiations with RTÉ, holding meeting after meeting, back and forth over several months, without resolution. During this time, however, I developed a deep affection for the two orchestras. The head of the Irish Federation of Musicians and Allied Professions at the time was a man called Jack Flahive, and because technically we were negotiating all of this under the aegis of the IFMAP, Jack came to all the meetings in RTÉ. Jack was a lovely man; he'd been a famous bandleader at one stage. He was stalwart in his support for me; as he lived in Shankill, he used to travel home with me after meetings, and we became good friends. I enjoyed my role in that case in every way. Apart from the claim itself, the process demystified orchestras for me: I learned how an orchestra is assembled.

Finally, we ended up in the Labour Court; the court's recommendation was that the musicians be given a 20 percent pay increase (this was the 1980s!), to be paid in two tranches, of 8 percent and 12 percent. An agreement was also reached on productivity: in the event, this didn't involve playing faster but took account of some changes in work practices which had been implemented in the previous couple of years, along with some new commitments.

I clearly remember the ballot in the Concert Hall on the Labour Court recommendation. I stood at the conductor's podium, explaining the settlement. It was the only time I have ever conducted an orchestra!

Of course, that was only one of many ballots I had to conduct during my years with the Transport Union. It is not an easy position to be in. The job of a union official is to get the best deal possible for the members, and to bring negotiations to a conclusion. Then it is back to the members to ask them to approve the deal. It is almost inevitable that someone will not be happy with what is being offered. Presenting the case to members can sometimes be quite delicate, and is never helped when those who have had no involvement in the negotiations start offering their opinions from the outside.

That is why, during the early part of 2010, I refrained from becoming an advocate for the Croke Park agreement on public sector pay and reform. This brought a fair degree of criticism down on my head – in some cases, I have to say, from people who had no experience at all of industrial relations, or indeed of any form of negotiations. As an opposition leader, I had no role in negotiating the deal. Yet I was being asked to interfere in the ballot. Political interference in the ballot process would have been very unwise, and indeed disrespectful of those who were being balloted, and who were entitled to space to make their own decision.

Ultimately, the musicians balloted to accept the Labour Court recommendation, and I thought that would be the end of it. But no: things began to go wrong. I got a call from Joan Miley to tell me that RTÉ weren't paying the award. (Apparently, a pay embargo had been imposed by the government right across the state sector, and RTÉ was instructed not to pay the award.)

Joan Miley, along with one or two other members of the committee, came into the office and told me that they were going to need my help again. I had to tell them that there was nothing more I could do, and reminded them that they weren't members of the ITGWU any more. At this point, they said: 'Well, could we become members of the union?' Now, this really was a minefield. Sometimes, groups of members do move between unions, but it can cause enormous friction, including the possibility of a complaint being lodged with the Irish Congress of Trade Unions. It was not the sort of thing that I wanted to have on my hands, and at that time I wasn't exactly in favour in the upper floors of Liberty Hall. The senior positions in the union are decided by election, and I had supported the losing team.

I told Joan and her colleagues that I didn't want to get into this. I explained the rules, which at the time stipulated that for a group of workers to move between unions, 80 percent must be in agreement. I hoped that this would be enough of a deterrent. It wasn't:

thanks to Joan, almost everyone signed on the line.

However, when I attempted to register the musicians as members of my branch, Head Office ordained that they should be allocated to a different branch. But Joan was having none of it. She rang one of the union's senior officers, and the applications were back on my desk within a few hours.

Joan's concern for her colleagues was all the more impressive because of the difficulties she encountered herself. Joan had joined the NSO in 1948, the year it was established. Later, in the early 1950s, she married another musician in the orchestra. Because of the marriage ban, she was required to resign her permanent job, but she was kept on, and so continued to play full-time, on a casual basis. She never stopped playing, apart from a period from 1954 to 1967, when she lived in various countries with her husband, and she played with the same commitment even after her husband passed away. In the early 1970s, new legislation was brought in by the coalition government, and married women were finally able to officially rejoin the workforce. Joan's problem, however, was that her pension entitlement was seriously reduced. After a long struggle, she eventually retired in 1996 with her pension, but her case demonstrates the absolute unfairness of the marriage ban.

I loved my work in the ITGWU. I got enormous job satisfaction from negotiating and solving problems. My attitude was – and still is – that there is a solution to every problem, no matter how intractable it might seem.

I also learned a lot about business, and about the economy. My job as a union official exposed me to a wide range of industries and types of employment. I learned the factors which overseas companies look for when considering locating in Ireland – and what is needed to keep them here. I learned about the continuing challenges faced by Irish industry to compete in the international marketplace. And because I represented managers, I developed an appreciation of how difficult it can be to run an enterprise and to manage people effectively.

I was greatly saddened by the circumstances in which I ended up leaving the ITGWU. In 1989, I was elected to the Dáil for the first time, alongside another new Workers' Party TD and ITGWU official, Pat Rabbitte. As we celebrated our election success, the union sent letters of dismissal and our P45s by courier to our homes. Previously, union employees who were elected to the Dáil were granted leave of absence for a period of time, and didn't have to immediately resign their jobs, but the union had decided to reverse this policy when Pat and I were elected. But we were determined not to take it lying down. A few days later, we mounted a picket – on Liberty Hall! I am happy to say that we received a lot of support from fellow members of staff, and from many individual members of the union. Many of those supporting us were Labour Party members who, even if we were not on the same team at the time, were anxious to see fairness prevail. I had worked hard for the union, and I was very sore at the time about the shabby way we had been treated. But all of that is a long time ago now, and it didn't change my basic attitude to trade unions.

I think people should be free to join a trade union. When we buy a house, we engage a solicitor to ensure that the contract is right. We engage an architect to make sure that the structure is sound. Similarly, we may seek the advice of a mechanic if we decide to buy a second-hand car. When we are offered an employment contract, isn't it reasonable to expect that we should be able to engage professional help in order to help us make a decision as to whether we should acept it? People question the value of trade union membership, and whether employees should be in a trade union. They seem to think that there is something wrong with the idea that we would get somebody who is professionally equipped to have a look at the employment contract and to advise about it and, if necessary, to go and talk with the employer.

The fundamental point is that an employee has a right to have professional representation in respect of their employment contract. Sometimes that is done collectively, although in a lot of cases now it's done individually, because contracts of employment are made on an individual basis.

When someone comes into my constituency office and tells me they've lost their job, I ask them if they are a member of a union. They say they aren't, and I ask them why. 'Well, because there is no union', they say, or 'The employer doesn't allow a union'. At this point, I say to myself: 'Well hold on a second, why should it be the employer's right to decide that for you?' An employee doesn't tell the employer whether or not the employer can be a member of a business association. The person who sells you a house doesn't tell you that you can't go to a solicitor. In the overwhelming majority of cases, being a member of a trade union is used by most trade union members simply to get advice or information on what they are entitled to.

There has been some comment about the Labour Party's relationship with the trade unions. Compared to other social-democratic parties in Europe, the links in Ireland between the Labour Party and trade unions are pretty limited: the financial contribution that the unions make to Labour amount to only about 5 percent of our annual income, whereas it can be as high as 60 percent in other countries.

The biggest single election donor in this year's US congressional elections is a public service trade union, which has made huge financial contributions to the Democrats. In the recent British Labour Party leadership election, the unions had one-third of the votes. That could not happen in Ireland because unions have no say at all in the election of a Labour leader; no say in the selection of Labour candidates; and no reserved seats on the Party's executive.

The links between the party and the unions are historical. The Labour Party grew out of an initiative taken by Connolly and Larkin, at the Trade Union Congress in 1912, to set up a party that would give political voice to the needs of working people. Over time, the Labour Party has evolved into something far more than that, and has broadened its appeal. Still, we are proud of the ties of history between the Labour Party and the Labour movement.

I don't think it is any secret that the relationship between the party and the unions came under some strain during the years of social partnership. As a trade union official, I supported the move in the late 1980s back to national wage agreements and social partnership. For the Labour Party in opposition, however, the fact that unions were cutting deals with Fianna Fáil in government introduced a certain strain into the relationship – a strain which, to be fair, both sides have openly acknowledged. This wasn't so much of a problem when social partnership was largely about a pay deal, but it became more problematic as more and more areas of economic and social policy came under the partnership umbrella. In their dealings with the government, the unions had to get the best possible deal for their members, but as an opposition party Labour was, and is, entitled to have a view on how it would like to see policy develop.

I have made it clear, on numerous occasions, that a Labour government would not be a trade union government, but a government of all the people. Labour in government will have to deal with the unions in the same way as they deal with any other group in Irish society – without fear or favour. At the same time, I believe that, in a small country like Ireland, social partnership, or social dialogue of some sort, has an important role to play. In the economic crisis in which we find ourselves, talking is a far better way of dealing with tensions than open conflict. We can't go back to the 'mission creep' of past social-partnership deals, but there is, I believe, a role for agreements that bring people with you. In a crisis such as the current one, Ireland's capacity to come together, and to work out solutions that people will stick with, can be a major asset to us all. That being said, we must avoid the problems of previous deals, which left too many people outside the room, looking in.

In the end, I remember Joan for her qualities, not just as a union representative, but also as a human being. She came out of an era when the domain of women was seen as the home, not the workplace. Yet Joan was dogged, determined, honest and forthright. She could also relieve a heightened, serious moment with her sparkling sense of humour. She rose to be president of the section committee of her union and for a time served on its national executive. She was independent-minded and resolute, and possessed great moral courage. We will always need such people in the battles we fight, whether small or large, against unfairness and inequality.

7

Proinsias De Rossa

I was very surprised when Proinsias De Rossa asked me if I would be interested in standing as a candidate in a general election. I had watched the emergence of Proinsias as a significant political figure in what was then Sinn Féin the Workers' Party and was greatly encouraged by his election as a TD for Dublin North West in February 1982. The surprise invitation was extended to me at a function in Finglas in early 1982 to celebrate his success. Some of my friends had campaigned for Proinsias in that election, and they invited me along to the celebration party a week or two later. I had never spoken to Proinsias before, though I had seen him at *ard fheiseanna* and at various other meetings, and he had, of course, contested elections before that. I had followed how well he had done in the previous election in June 1981, and then his successful campaign in February 1982. I was a member of the Workers' Party then, but not a very active one; I simply didn't have much time to devote to party business. I was in the DIY phase of my life, assembling my own furniture! I had recently got married, and was in a job, as branch secretary with the Transport and General Workers' Union, that required me to travel all around the country.

Therefore, I was surprised when, in the course of our first, brief conversation, Proinsias suggested that I consider running for election myself. At the time, I passed it off as a nice, flattering thing to say to a young guy; it was certainly not something I took very seriously. However, shortly after that I became more active in Dun Laoghaire, attending the occasional local meeting. When another election was called, on 24 November that year, I found myself as the new Workers' Party candidate. It had been decided that the party would contest more seats in order to raise its profile and broaden its base. Proinsias contacted me again, and came to our constituency council meeting in Shanganagh Park House in Shankill in October. We were not a large organisation – there were probably about a dozen of us at the meeting – and we had never stood a candidate for a general election before. I accepted the nomination without any expectation that we would win a seat. I was going to give it a try, and thought it would be an interesting experience – though not one I expected to repeat!

That election was a very short, sharp campaign – though not as sharp as the grim November weather. In the end, I got around 1,300 votes; I also learned some things about myself, and about running for election. The first was that I loved canvassing. I loved getting out and talking to people, hearing their stories and getting their opinions; and I loved the buzz of the election itself, even when it was time for the count. I also learned that anything can happen in a campaign: more people came on board to support us, and by the end we had quite a sizeable organisation. To campaign with no expectation of winning was, of course, quite liberating: it left me free to enjoy the experience. The point of the outing was to raise the profile of the party in that constituency, which we succeeded in doing. However, enjoyable as it was, my forays into the battlefield of elected politics were to be put on hold for a few years. There was more furniture to assemble: my daughter Gráinne was born in 1982, and Oisín arrived in 1985.

Still, from that election on, I became more active locally. In part, this was because once you put your name on a ballot paper, people in the area know that you are politically engaged. This makes it more likely that you will be invited to local meetings: I found myself involved to an increasing extent in residents' associations and community organisations. The next local elections were in 1985, and I stood for the council in the Ballybrack electoral area. Once again, I didn't have any great expectations, but I did go out to win, and gave it my best shot. I think I surprised even myself by getting elected, after a recount, to Dun Laoghaire Borough Council and Dublin County Council.

I came into more regular contact with Proinsias De Rossa after becoming a local councillor. He was one of three Workers' Party TDs who were elected to the Dáil in 1982; he became my sounding board, a conduit for issues or questions I felt needed to be raised in the Dáil. Over time, we became very good friends. Throughout the

1980s, Proinsias was consistently articulating what I felt about those big issues about which debate was raging in Ireland at the time: personal freedom, the liberalisation of Irish society, efforts to tackle poverty and disadvantage, and the commitment to democracy. I was experiencing my own political evolution, through being elected in the local elections in 1985, standing in the general election of 1987, and finally being elected to the Dáil in 1989, when I became Proinsias's parliamentary colleague.

Proinsias succeeded Tomás MacGiolla as president of the Workers' Party. As the new leader, he set out to modernise and democratise the party, and to move it to a more mainstream social-democratic position. He wanted to leave behind all kinds of left-wing jargon, and to communicate our politics in the everyday language of the people we represented.

I supported him strongly in all this, but his reforms inevitably met with resistance. In February 1992, Proinsias moved to reconstitute the Workers' Party and to overhaul its organisation. However, at a special conference held in the Royal Marine Hotel in Dun Laoghaire, he failed, by a handful of votes, to secure the two-thirds majority he required in order to implement his proposals. By that stage, the damage was done. The differences had become irreconcilable, and I joined Proinsias in leaving the Workers' Party and forming Democratic Left.

A number of things impressed me about Proinsias. First of all, I admire his personal modesty. He has been a very influential figure in Irish politics, but at the same time he is quite a shy person, very modest, gentle and quiet – a rare combination in politics. He is also someone who has shown great courage to overcome a stammer, which would normally be a major handicap for somebody who has to speak often in public, as politicians do. He is unquestionably a politician of conviction, and the strength of his convictions has not abated with the passing of the years. Throughout the 1980s, he took strong positions on various controversial, unpopular issues – positions that were informed by his principles, and certainly not by political calculation. In the early 1980s, for example, as the country was convulsed by bitter debates about abortion, he was one of the few politicians who opposed the so-called 'pro-life' amendment. He was also an early campaigner for the right to divorce, and the right to access contraception. For me, his most decisive role was in tackling poverty. As Minister for Social Welfare in the rainbow government 1994–97, he spearheaded Ireland's first anti-poverty strategy, and introduced a system of 'poverty-proofing' government policy, to ensure that it did not inadvertently worsen the conditions of the least well-off.

On Northern Ireland, Proinsias was ahead of his time: a republican who rejected armed struggle. He was talking about a settlement in Northern Ireland that would respect both traditions, at a time when most politicians in the Republic were still wilfully blinded by the green flag. He believed firmly that the unionist, Protestant, loyalist tradition had to be respected, and that it was neither possible, nor ethical, to coerce a million Northern Protestants into becoming part of a united Ireland against their will.

Any successful settlement, therefore, had to be based on mutual respect. He was also strongly opposed to the use of violence, and abhorred what the Provisional IRA was doing in Northern Ireland. Even when others had tired of a conflict that had become increasingly entrenched, Proinsias never wavered in his commitment to finding a resolution to the problem.

Proinsias De Rossa was, and is, a democrat. He strongly believes in parliamentary democracy and democratic institutions, and in the importance of building on them, improving them and defending them. That belief shaped his politics in relation to Northern Ireland, and it continues to drive his politics as a member of the European Parliament. Proinsias first stood for the European Parliament in 1989, when he polled more than seventy thousand votes in Dublin. It was the party's best electoral performance, and an excellent campaign, with significant contributions from Eoghan Harris and the artist Brian Maguire. However, he had recently taken over the leadership of the party, and it was difficult to combine membership of both the Dáil and the European Parliament. Internal divisions were emerging in the Workers' Party, and he was needed back in Ireland; he resigned as an MEP, and his seat was filled by Des Geraghty. However, it was clear to me that Proinsias was deeply interested in European politics, and what was happening there. Since then, he has always been a hugely committed European parliamentarian. The battle for ideas excites him: and you can't beat the European Union as an example of the phenomenal power of an idea.

For all its prosaic beginnings as the European Coal and Steel

Community, the concept of a unified Europe, and a common market, could only have been dreamed up by idealists. The Treaty of Rome emerged from the ashes of Europe in the aftermath of the Second World War. These were countries – France and Germany mainly, but also the Benelux countries and Italy – which had already fought each other twice in protracted, bloody wars in the first half of the twentieth century. Many of those who first worked together on the project of European unity had painful memories of the Second World War, which had only ended a few years previously, yet they were determined to come together to pursue a common agenda. In the end, they instigated the most successful peace process in history, and Europe reaped an enormous economic dividend.

As well as producing the first generation of twentieth-century Europeans not to have lived through war, the European Union has transformed the quality of life of those countries that have joined it. Spain, Portugal and Greece were just emerging from long, Fascist dictatorships in the 1970s, and their becoming part of the European Union helped secure their futures as peaceful democracies. When Ireland joined the Common Market in 1973, the average income here was less than two-thirds of what it was in the rest of Europe. By contrast, in 2009, Irish incomes were 128 percent of the EU average. Some of the enormous benefits of European Union membership for Ireland are measurable in material terms: €60 billion in EU funding for agriculture, community projects and infrastructure, and easy access to the European market, which has helped attract to these shores almost a thousand foreign companies, half of which are from other EU member states. There are other huge benefits to EU membership: the progress we have made on equality, the improved quality of our environment, and the cultural exchange and openness that comes from the freedom to travel, work and study in the twenty-seven countries of the EU.

About two years ago, I sat with Proinsias at a seminar in Liberty Hall on the changes that were taking place in employment law at European level. I was greatly impressed by his command of the law, including its finer details. People sometimes see EU politics and legislation as being quite remote from their lives, but the hall that day was alive with discussion and engagement. It was packed with shop stewards, lawyers and other interested people from all over the country. Proinsias talked with ease about this important but very complex subject, to an interested audience. It was fascinating to watch people relating their experience of employment legislation in their workplaces in Ireland to what was happening in the European Parliament in Strasbourg.

What the debates about the Lisbon Treaty referendum in Ireland, particularly the first referendum in 2008, demonstrated was that the disconnect between Irish citizens and what goes on in the European Union is simultaneously large, and false. The forum on employment law I attended with Proinsias could be replicated with regard to environmental legislation, agriculture, women's rights, climate change and consumers' rights. So why, in the course of a referendum campaign, was there so much focus on fear – on what the EU could potentially 'take away' from Ireland – rather than on how membership of the EU benefits us? One of the reasons for this, of course, is that the only time we have a public debate about our membership is during a referendum campaign – which is, by its very nature, antagonistic. Most of the blame for this situation, however, lies at the feet of Irish politicians, who have taken a somewhat disingenuous approach to Ireland's relationship with the EU. Since 1973, generations of politicians have taken credit for the EU funds that have flowed into Ireland but have blamed the EU for any unpopular decisions! This is despite the fact that no decision at EU level that affects Ireland in a significant way is taken without an Irish government minister in the room. Changes introduced by the Lisbon Treaty will give the Dáil greater power to scrutinise these decisions – meaning that it will also be able to hold ministers to account more effectively for what happens in council meetings in Brussels. However, the onus must also be on government ministers to be upfront about the compromises that are inevitably part and parcel of being a member of a twenty-seven-strong group of states.

One of the reasons I suspect that being an MEP so suits Proinsias is because he is a truly dedicated internationalist. For him, ensuring that the basic rights of people in Palestine, or workers in South America, or children in India are respected, is as important as protecting those same rights for people in Ireland and the wider European Union. Of course, internationalism is an important part of the social-democratic tradition. For the Labour Party, as for our sister parties elsewhere, solidarity beyond our national borders is a core value: Ireland is the seventh-largest donor of overseas development assistance per head of population in the world; we have a proud tradition of peacekeeping with the UN; generations of Irish missionaries worked as educators and medics in some of the poorest parts of the globe. In these things, Ireland punches above its diplomatic weight.

We should do more to capitalise on both our existing strengths, and our natural advantages as an island nation in the EU. Should we, for example, become a logistics hub for international emergency relief aid? As a country with a number of deep ports, good international transport connections, and substantial experience in logistics among both civilians and the defence forces, could we not become a world depot for emergency relief supplies. We should also use our influence more effectively within the UN and the EU to address some of the structural causes of global poverty, such as trade rules and, increasingly, the effects of climate change, and to press for an international 'Robin Hood' tax on global financial transactions. (Such a tax would raise about €400 billion a year, or about three times the total amount the world currently spends on aid.)

*

Proinsias is one of the most respected members of the European Parliament. He was born in north Dublin, and worked in his parents' greengrocery business as a child. He became involved in republican politics as a teenager, and later became interested in Ireland's various social problems, including poverty and substandard housing. In the 1960s, Proinsias became involved in the housing action committees in Dublin; this involvement radicalised his politics and laid the foundations for his lifelong commitment to social justice.

I have always thought of Proinsias as a kindred spirit. He mirrors how I think in many ways, and we have become close friends outside of politics. Without a doubt, his biggest influence on me was encouraging me to become involved in electoral politics in the first place. When he first asked me, all those years ago, to do so, it was no more than a straw in the wind: I doubt whether he remembers that brief conversation. Little did I suspect then how interwoven our political paths would become. We were both involved in organising the first Peace Train. We both supported Mary Robinson's candidacy for the presidency from an early stage; indeed, we had some difficulty persuading some people in the Workers' Party to go along with it. We both served as ministers in the rainbow government of 1994–97, with Labour and Fine Gael.

Following the defeat of that government in the general election of 1997, the conversation began about the future for the Labour Party, and for Democratic Left. Did it make sense to have two left-of-centre parties, with almost identical political programmes, competing for the same political space? Both parties had campaigned together for agreed candidates in two presidential elections; we had served in government together, pursuing common policies; we had soldiered together to get the divorce referendum over the line in 1996; and the two of us had generally come to the conclusion that there was little that separated us.

Talk about closer co-operation was tentative and informal at first. However, both Proinsias and Ruairi Quinn, who became leader of the Labour Party in 1997, recognised the potential for such co-operation. They nominated Brendan Howlin and me to lead discussions at a more formal level.

Brendan and I shared a conviction that it was necessary – and, just as important, possible – to amalgamate the two parties into a single social-democratic party, and that we should try to make this new party the leading force in Irish politics. There was no reason, other than the historic baggage of the Civil War, why Ireland – a modern state – could not have a large Labour Party, capable of winning a general election and leading a government. If we could put our energies into working together, instead of competing against each other, we would be serving our cause much better.

'The sum will be greater than the parts' was our mantra in seeking to persuade reluctant members of both parties to go along with the merger. For a time, it was not entirely obvious that the sum *would* be greater than the parts, but there are few now who would question the success of the merger. Proinsias and Ruairi deserve great credit for the foresight and generosity they showed in what was sometimes a difficult process.

The Labour movement in Ireland had been dogged by division. The patriotic decision by Labour not to contest the 1918 general election damaged Labour's political growth, and the Civil War divided working people and progressives. The Labour Party split in the 1940s due to deep divisions in the trade union movement. For most of my lifetime, the Left in Ireland was fragmented and divided, with many left-wing politicians and party activists being more concerned about always being right than about being successful.

I admit that I, like many others, contributed to those divisions. But I have learned! Labour will not succeed unless we are united and disciplined. Now that we have achieved these things, there are strong signs that we can win, and lead the next government. Why not? Most people in Ireland share the values of Labour: that it is possible to build a prosperous, enterprise-led economy with a fair society, in a sustainable environment.

Faced with massive unemployment, and an economic crisis that has prompted a crisis in confidence in the country both at home and abroad, Ireland needs a Labour-led government now more than ever. And for the first time since independence, this is a credible prospect. However, it it important to note that it has become credible only because we have worked for it, and because we have learned the futility of being divided.

Looking back, it has been some journey since that winter's evening in February 1982, when Proinsias De Rossa, then a newly elected TD, suggested to me that I think about standing for election to the Dáil. At the time, I thought it was a daft idea!

Yet I have never regretted it. Every single day, I remind myself that the work which I do is on behalf of all the people who have voted me into this office. In a democracy, there is no greater honour or privilege than to be freely chosen by fellow citizens, to represent them in the national parliament.

8

Margaret Thatcher

I think we have gone through a period when too many children and people have been given to understand 'I have a problem, it is the government's job to cope with it!' or 'I have a problem, I will go and get a grant to cope with it!', 'I am homeless, the government must house me!' And so they are casting their problems on society, and who is society? There is no such thing! There are individual men and women and there are families, and no government can do anything except through people, and people look to themselves first.

But it went too far. If children have a problem, it is society that is at fault. *There is no such thing as society.* There is a living tapestry of men and women and people, and the beauty of that tapestry and the quality of our lives will depend upon how much each of us is prepared to take responsibility for ourselves, and how much each of us is prepared to turn around and help by our own efforts those who are unfortunate.

Extracts from an interview given by Prime Minister Margaret Thatcher for Woman's Own *magazine, published on 31 October 1987*

Margaret Thatcher may seem like a strange choice of subject for inclusion in a book about people who have influenced me. I include Mrs Thatcher for much the same reason that my favourite British newspaper is the *Daily Telegraph*: when I pick up the *Telegraph*, I know almost immediately what I'm up against.

When you are in the business of opinions, and taking a view of the world and of politics, it is sometimes useful to measure what you are *for* in terms of its polar opposite. It helps to clarify things. Margaret Thatcher, more than anybody, provides that foil for socialists and social democrats. Of course, it isn't enough to know what you are *against*. Rather, the clash of ideas, and robust debate, can often help to clarify what is strong and what is weak in terms of your own ideas, and make it possible to think more clearly about the future, and what really matters.

The starting point of my political viewpoint, of the social-democratic view of the world, is that there *is* such a thing as society. That is the simple notion that underpinned the bargain struck in practically every country in Western Europe in the aftermath of the Second World War. At that time, people saw the great wealth that could be created through industrialisation and an enterprise-based economy. They also recognised the great inequalities that could be produced in industrialised countries, and the terrible consequences of strife between left and right, which had given rise to totalitarian regimes in Germany, Italy and Russia.

The solution adopted in western Europe was a sort of social-democratic bargain. A recognition that none of us is an island, and that we have to combine an enterprise-based economy with fairness and mutual support. There was significant state intervention in providing social supports and stimulating economic activity, along with substantial regulation of the private sector. This strategy was underpinned by Keynesian economic theory, which was still dominant when I was a student of economics in the mid 1970s.

This social-democratic approach underpinned the long post-war economic boom in Europe, known to economists as 'the golden age', which endured until the oil crises of the 1970s. When Mrs Thatcher came to power in Britain in 1979, and Ronald Reagan in the USA in 1980, they started systematically to dismantle the whole model. Both were inspired by thinkers such as the monetarist economist Milton Friedman. Under their direction, monetarism became the new dominant economic ideology. Politically and philosophically, the neo-liberal thinker Friedrich Hayek was a major inspiration for Thatcher – to the point where she once banged a copy of one of his books on a table and declared: 'This is what we believe!'

What she believed – and set about implementing – was that the world would move away from the notion of society being at the core of human existence. Thatcher's view was that freedom equated to freedom of the market: that, as she said, there are individuals, and families, and businesses, but there is no such thing as society, and that the market will determine everything. At the same time, and perhaps somewhat paradoxically, she was responsible for centralising political power around herself: if you wanted to free the market, she believed, you needed to concentrate power in order to do so.

Her thinking, and that of other neo-liberals, has dominated politics around the world for the last thirty years, and has played a key role in bringing about the current global economic crisis. The idea that markets should be free and unfettered has been proven to be ruinous, particularly for the poor, and especially for Ireland.

The philosophy propagated so fiercely by Thatcher came to dominate thinking here. In many respects, the Progressive Democrats, who were formed in 1985, were an early manifestation of Irish Thatcherism. Of course, the domestic political circumstances that gave rise to the formation of the PDs was the antipathy to Charles Haughey within Fianna Fáil, but the economic philosophy they adopted was Thatcher's. Others who opposed Haughey, but who stayed in Fianna Fáil, including Charlie McCreevy and the late Seamus Brennan, were notable for their embrace of Thatcherite thinking.

Changes in the housing and banking sectors show what free-market dogma, combined with naked greed on the part of a 'golden circle', was to mean for Ireland. In the late 1990s, when property price started to go up, I was the Labour Party spokesperson on housing. As the rise in house prices became more and more dramatic, I convened a group of experts, chaired by Professor P. J. Drudy of Trinity College, to look at the issue and advise the party on how to tackle it. The report made a series of detailed recommendations, based on a set of core political principles. These principles included the idea that housing is not just a commodity, it is also an essential human need – which means that society, in this case government, has an essential role to play in regulating the market and reining in the rise in house prices. If hard-working families cannot afford a home, the market simply isn't working.

The Fianna Fáil-led government ignored these arguments, sticking to the view that the market would correct the situation by increasing supply. Labour's repeated proposals to control the price of building land were rebuffed with spurious claims about the constitutionality of our proposals. I recall Bobby Molloy, the PD Minister for Housing, dismissing Labour's proposals to control house prices as 'Communistic [sic]'. Of course, Fianna Fáil's connections to property developers, displayed annually in the infamous 'Galway tent', influenced this thinking, but it can also be linked back to Thatcher's political philosophy.

Meanwhile, and with disastrous consequences for the world economy and for Ireland, the Thatcherite doctrine of light-touch regulation for financial services was spreading across the globe. In Ireland, Fianna Fáil interpreted 'light-touch' to mean very little touch at all, and the foundations were laid for a banking crisis that, at the time of writing, has brought Ireland to the brink of national bankruptcy.

One of the tragedies of our economic collapse is that it could have been averted. The period of greatest prosperity in this country was from the mid-1990s until the crash of 2008. Suppose that this period had not been driven, as it was, by economic right-wingers? Suppose the rainbow coalition had been re-elected in 1997? I believe that Ireland would be a much better place today.

During the boom, those influenced by Thatcherite thinking claimed that the dramatic economic growth that we experienced was the direct result of Charlie McCreevy's tax cuts and what they would see as the freeing up of the market. I would counter by saying that the boom was already well under way in 1997 – the product of a competitive, export-driven economy. When Labour left office, the public finances were back in the black and the country was creating a thousand jobs a week. If that growth had been managed differently over the decade since, we would not be in our current mess. Even in the run-in to the 2002 election, house prices were starting to stabilise – until Fianna Fáil put their foot down hard on the accelerator again. Without the long period of Fianna Fáil-led government, I doubt that we would have ended up with the property bubble; and we would have had a stronger, better infrastructure, a better education system, a better health system, and better social services: in short, a better society. In 1997, however, Thatcher's view of the world prevailed in Ireland.

*

Margaret Thatcher first came into my consciousness as the education secretary in the Heath government in Britain, which ran from 1970 to 1974. At the time, I was becoming involved in student politics, and we had considerable contact with the National Union of Students in Britain. Thatcher had withdrawn free milk in schools, and the NUS organised a campaign against her decision. She came to be known as 'Thatcher the Snatcher'; the campaign slogan was 'Some cows give milk'!

In 1974, after Labour had won the general election, she challenged Edward Heath for the leadership of the Conservative Party. To the surprise of many commentators, she succeeded in replacing him. Even though Thatcher was surrounded by right-wing ideologues like Keith Joseph, the same commentators would have been even more surprised had they known that she would achieve such dominance over British politics, and the direction of world affairs, for so long.

An early indication of her style, and her impact on Ireland, came in her mishandling of the H-Block hunger strikes. More than anybody, Thatcher was responsible for the rise of Sinn Féin because of her inflexible, insensitive and uncompassionate approach to the hunger strikers. Ed Moloney's book, *A Secret History of the IRA*, among others on the same subject, makes it clear that there was a mood among the prisoners themselves to have a settlement. What stopped this happening was, firstly, Thatcher's inflexibility, and secondly, an apparent desire on the part of Sinn Féin to keep the strike going in order to win electoral support. It is instructive to compare Thatcher's approach with that of Tony Blair's Labour government in the late 1990s. On the one hand, you have Thatcher's complete inflexibility, and then on the other you have the willingness of the Labour government to engage, and to compromise.

Her premiership might have come to an end at the 1983 election had it not been for the Falklands war. The most striking, and brutally honest, quote I remember from that time was that of Neil Kinnock, who later became the Labour Party leader. In the course of an interview, somebody put it to him: doesn't the prime minister, Mrs Thatcher, have guts? He replied: 'Well, it's a pity that so many young men had to leave their guts in Goose Green in order to prove it.' This comment was, of course, roundly criticised as being lacking in taste, but it was a very powerful – and accurate – assessment of the situation. She went on to win a landslide victory in the general election.

In her second term in office, she really began to define the Thatcherite agenda, both in terms of policies like privatisation, and in key political moments, the most important of which was the miners' strike of 1984. To understand the significance, and the tragedy, of the miners' strike, we have to remind ourselves of what Britain was like in the late 1970s, when Thatcher came to power. Under James Callaghan's Labour government of 1976–79, there was widespread industrial unrest, and serious problems in the trade union movement. There were several occasions where workplaces, such as the big car manufacturers, would be shut down by strike action, following a show of hands at a mass meeting in a car park. There were many of these spontaneous, 'wild-cat' strikes, as they were called, culminating in the 'winter of discontent', which undermined the Labour government and played into the hands of Thatcher's conservatives. This period left a deep scar on the collective memory of the British electorate.

Thatcher did her utmost to curtail the power of the trade unions through legislation limiting their scope for action – some of which was simple common sense, such as requiring a ballot before a strike. The real reckoning with the trade unions, however, came in 1984, when she picked a fight with the most powerful of the unions, the National Union of Mineworkers. The union itself had its own internal issues. The NUM's fiercely anti-communist president, Joe Gormley, remained on in office until his likely successor, Mick MacGahey, who led the miners in Scotland, was, under the union's rules, too old to succeed him. Gormley was replaced instead by Arthur Scargill.

Thatcher was looking for a fight, and the NUM leadership walked into it. On my first day as a trade union official, we were addressed by Michael Mullen, then the general secretary of the Irish Transport and General Workers' Union. He wanted to convey to us the rudiments of what it meant to be a good trade union official. He summed this up in two pieces of advice. The first was that we should never tell lies to members. This created a certain amount of amusement among some of the more long-serving officials, because it was generally believed that Micky was a little challenged himself on that front! But we all took the second piece of advice seriously: never organise an ice-cream strike in the middle of winter!

Equally, you don't call a coal strike in the spring, and you don't organise a strike at all when the employer – in this case the government – is ready for you. Arthur Scargill failed to follow either of these rules: he called his members out on strike in March.

Thatcher and her people were prepared for the strike. In the conflict that followed, the miners, who were trying to protect their jobs and their communities, were caught up in a clash of ideologies between Scargill, on one hand, and Thatcher on the other. She won, and set about laying waste to Britain's industrial communities: the north, the midlands and Wales in particular. Some such clash between the miners and the government was, perhaps, inevitable at some stage, but the ultimate result of the conflict, and the way it was played out, was deeply damaging to many mining communities across the country. There could certainly have been a more managed winding-down period and a more managed transition from mining to other forms of activity than actually took place. It has taken a generation for those communities to recover; indeed, many of them have not recovered at all.

As with the Falklands, Kinnock, who had succeeded Michael Foot as Labour Party leader after the 1983 general election, was faced with an impossible dilemma in dealing with the miners' strike. His sympathies were clearly with the miners, who were caught up in the battle between Scargill and Thatcher. It was just one of several moments that highlighted the difficulties faced by a party that was torn between its emotional attachment to the traditions and values of the Labour movement, and the need to learn, adapt, modernise and move ahead.

When Thatcher came to office, the British Labour Party was deeply divided; those divisions broke open in the period after they lost the 1979 election and, of course, ultimately the party split.

What could be called the right wing of the party broke away, led by a group of defectors who came to be known as the 'Gang of Four': Shirley Williams, William Rodgers, David Owen and Roy Jenkins. They founded the Social Democratic Party, or SDP, in 1981. Shirley Williams was a principled and progressive politician, and had a fine record as education secretary: the Labour Party ought to have been able to keep people like her within the fold, but she left after what was a kind of left-wing coup. The hard left insisted that by driving the Labour Party further to the left, it would progress. It didn't; in fact, the party failed miserably to offer a credible opposition to Thatcher and the Tories. In the 1983 election, she inflicted a heavy defeat on them: it was their worst-ever election performance. The hard lesson for Labour was that if you want to have a political party that can win power, you have to build a broad church.

After that election, the Labour leader, Michael Foot, stood down. Though he was a man of great intellect, and a gifted writer, whom I admired and who enjoyed enormous respect, the party he left behind was floundering. When Neil Kinnock became leader, he immediately took on the Trotskyites – the so-called 'militant tendency' – which had become in effect a party within a party. Kinnock confronted the Trotskyites, and ultimately drove them out of the party, as he began to broaden Labour's appeal. Slowly, Labour's fortunes started to recover.

Ultimately, the politics of the hard left are self-defeating. It's all very well to keep the spirit of rebellion alive, to keep the protests going, and to maintain everybody in a permanent state of agitation, in the hope that the revolution is going to happen someday. In the real world, however, you must allow some time for people to take a breather, consolidate the gains that have been made, and then move on from there. Len Murray, who was general secretary of the British TUC from 1973 to 1984, once said of the Left's hard-line attitude – of holding out until all demands are met – that 'little fish are sweet'. What he meant was that small, incremental gains are sometimes just as worthwhile as well as major shifts. The early 1980s represented a huge defeat for working people and the Labour movement in Britain. Taking extreme-left positions which may sound very appealing to left-wing insiders doesn't bring much tangible benefit to those who are poor and disadvantaged – whom the Left claims to represent.

The period was a disaster for the British Labour Party and produced nearly two decades of Tory rule. It led to a redefinition and reorientation of politics in Britain, and arguably in the rest of Europe as well. It certainly influenced the direction and the pace of politics here in Ireland.

For a long period in the three decades that followed the election of Margaret Thatcher, the Left fumbled the ideological battle. With the rise of Thatcher and the end of communism, her ideology, not theirs, became the dominant economic outlook. Everything centred on promoting markets, weakening regulation, and reducing the size of the state, and its role in economic activity. We on the left largely failed to challenge that agenda effectively – until recently, as the old ways of doing things have been shown to fail. In order for

economies to survive, not only does there have to be state involvement, but the state has had to take the lead in dealing with problems
such as the banking crisis and in generating the conditions to create
employment. So this is the first lesson to be learnt from Thatcher:
that we have to fight for what we stand for; that we are not just individuals in an atomised world but are part of a society. We are inter-
dependent, as people, as communities, and as countries.

We also have to stand up for the idea of equality. In their recent
best-seller *The Spirit Level*, Richard Wilkinson and Kate Pickett,
both professors of epidemiology, show that more equal societies are
better societies – and, crucially, not just for people who are poor.
They are better for everybody because there is less crime, better standards of health, and a better quality of life. People who believe in
progressive politics must fight for the idea that this is the way in
which societies should be run, with equality as the guiding torch.

Thatcher's statement about there being no such thing as society
encapsulates the defining idea which separates Right from Left in
the larger battle of ideas. It's the best statement of what the politics
of the Right is all about. Everything is focused on the individual; we
provide for ourselves. This viewpoint is very strong in some aspects
of American life and culture, expressed in issues such as the debate
over the right to bear arms. In Ireland, we saw this kind of thinking
too, albeit expressed in different ways. One feature of the property
boom in Ireland, for example, was the proliferation over the last
decade of gated housing estates. At the height of the boom, we were
creating new ghettos at both ends of the social spectrum.

The same 'no such thing as society' approach drove Charlie McCreevy's tax-cutting agenda: put the money in people's pockets, and let individuals spend it. I understand that, and I believe in max-imising our individual economic freedom, but we also have to address the question of how to provide for ourselves together – how we live together, and interact with each other. We must always nur-ture and restate the solidarity that exists between us.

Of course, society does not always have to mean the state. One of the reasons why Thatcher was so successful in her assault on social democracy was that the Left had come to identify society with the state, or government, as though they were one and the same thing. This was not always the case: the early pioneers of social democracy had wanted to encourage and promote different ways of bringing people together to act collectively. It was only after the horrendous experience of the Second World War that the Left's notion of collec-tive action became associated to an increasing extent with the state. This was a mistake, both because it opened an opportunity for Thatcher and Reagan to demonise the failures of 'big government', with which the Left was almost exclusively associated, and also because there will always be limits to what the state can achieve.

The current Conservative Party leader, David Cameron, is Thatcher's ideological successor in many ways; he has been clever in the way that he has tackled the relationship between the state and society. In promoting what he calls 'the big society', he is arguing that government doesn't work very well, and that, anyway, there is only so much that government can do. So, instead, he argues that the size of government should be reduced and that 'society' should fill the gap (as though government was somehow not part of society). Cameron is cleverly distancing himself from Thatcher, and her argument that there is no such thing as society, while still arguing for a smaller state. In fact, Cameron's 'big society' is an attempt to appropriate the language of the Left, and make it his own, in the interests of what is essentially an individualist agenda. It would be a mistake to let him do so, just as it would be a mistake to fall back on the argument that society and the state are one and the same thing.

For at least the next five years, governments across Europe will be deeply constrained in what they can achieve. In many countries, the state is now a far bigger player in the banking system that it ever wanted to be; the need to fend off another Great Depression has left many governments deeply indebted. As we enter an era of austerity, the Left needs, not to fall back on old mantras, but to be inventive in terms of the solutions it offers. There is more to society than the state. There are other ways in which we can come together to achieve collective goals – perhaps with the state as a partner, rather than as funder, provider and regulator. David Cameron's 'big society' is intended to serve a privileged few; our society can serve the needs of all of us.

In Ireland, our left-right divide has often been marked by social rather than economic issues: women's rights, contraception, family planning, divorce, equality legislation, and the issue of civil unions and civil partnerships. Now there is a broad consensus about most of these matters. To argue for a separation of church and state thirty years ago was very radical; now, few people would question it. The debate is now more on economic, or socio-economic, lines. Over the coming years, Ireland will have to rebuild its economy; the issue of economic fairness will once again come to the fore. If we accept that there is such a thing as society, that there is solidarity and interdependence and fairness, everything else, including prosperity, flows from this. The notion that somehow we have to chose between fairness and prosperity is simply false. Of course, there are areas where there are tensions between the two goals, but unless society lays down a solid foundation of services, such as health and education, and unless government plays its role in promoting innovation and enterprise, we will not be able to rebuild the economy.

Those who believe in the importance of developing a social-democratic society have to be clear about their political philosophy, but there is also an issue relating to the way in which we communicate the message. The British Labour Party had to modernise and broaden its appeal in order to reconnect with the public; it had to speak to Britain in the language of the times. In Ireland, the Labour Party has to listen to what its supporters – and its potential voters – are saying, and it has to respond to these concerns while remaining true to its principles. Our politics have to be clearly defined, but we also have to listen; it's not just about turning up on doorsteps at election time.

This is what we are trying to do. We are not Fianna Fáil, and we are not Fine Gael. We have a distinctive view of Ireland, of the world, and of the economy, and we pursue that vigorously. I think we can do so with a great deal of confidence because the values that underpin the Labour Party are values that are shared by the majority of people in this country. Most people believe in fairness and in social justice. Most people believe that work and enterprise should be rewarded, and that we have to have a prosperous economy. We can't share wealth unless we create it, and to achieve that you have to have successful businesses, people working in them, and the innovation that helps those businesses thrive, as the world around us changes.

The job of government is about managing economic activity while at the same time maintaining the fabric of society, and enforcing the rules that keep us together and provide the level playing field for business to operate on. That's our view. The Fianna Fáil view – or at least its practice – has been to get hand in glove with certain wealthy interests. The party didn't start out like that, but that is what it has become.

*

Margaret Thatcher was a revolutionary of the Right; she transformed Britain, including its politics. She shaped the economic firmament through the 1980s and 1990s, and into the present century. She was the main driver in creating what became a new economic consensus, centred around the idea that the state should not interfere in the market.

Part of me admires that, because politics needs people who are 'game-changers', people who challenge the status quo and are prepared to think about our problems differently. But I return to her statement about society. Are we just individuals in a marketplace? Or is there a public space, and a need for social provision? Should everything be commodified, broken down and sold, or do we thrive best when we balance individual freedom and enterprise with a capacity to work together to achieve common goals? Are we all to be left to sink or swim in the economic tide, or do we pull together, as 'one Ireland', to get through.

I only need to read that statement from Margaret Thatcher to feel assured once again of what I'm against, but also, more importantly, of what I'm for. There *is* such a thing as society.

9

T. K. Whitaker

Dr T. K. Whitaker will forever be associated with his groundbreaking economic report of 1958, which is largely credited with laying the foundation for Ireland's subsequent economic transformation. His influence on the life of this country, however, stretched well beyond those years. Whitaker represents all that is good about the public service, and embodies a kind of practical patriotism that we should all seek to emulate.

T. K. Whitaker was appointed Secretary of the Department of Finance in 1956 (today the position is known as Secretary General – the civil service head of the department). Whitaker was just thirty-nine at the time, marking this out as a highly unusual appointment, in an era when the normal civil service career path involved serving your time and moving up on the basis of seniority.

The 1950s was a dark time for Ireland, during which the country endured a slow-moving but profound economic crisis. After just over thirty years of independence, Ireland was afflicted by poverty and unemployment. The native industries that we still had were in decline, and tens of thousands of Irish people were taking the boat to England every year. In truth, the Ireland of that time was a conservative, depressing place; it was not a period to be romanticised in any way. The economic crisis was turning into a crisis of confidence, summed up by Whitaker himself in the following terms:

> The years 1955–56 had plumbed the depths of hopelessness. One of the recurring series of balance-of-payments crises was overcome, but only at the cost of stagnation, high unemployment and emigration. The mood of despondency was palpable. Something had to be done, or the achievement of national independence would prove to have been a futility.
>
> *from* Interests *by T. K. Whitaker (IPA, 1983)*

The government that appointed Whitaker was a coalition – the country's second inter-party government – comprised largely of Fine Gael and Labour. Whitaker, along with his team, which came to be known as 'the Whitaker Committee', began work on a strategy to address the crisis. Despite Fianna Fáil's return to office in March 1957, the committee was allowed to continue its work in order to reach its conclusions, under the new government. I am not at all sure that Fianna Fáil would allow such a thing to happen today. In 1958, Whitaker's report, entitled *Economic Development*, was published.

It is important to remember the context in which Whitaker and his committee wrote and published the report. It was towards the end of Éamon de Valera's long period at the helm of the Irish government, and he was still the dominant figure in politics, along with others, including Sean MacEntee and Frank Aiken, who had been among those who had founded Fianna Fáil. The same was true on the Fine Gael side. They were all individuals who had been at the centre of power for four decades, more or less, and were now old men – and they *were* mostly men, of course.

An important dimension of the independence struggle had been the argument that Ireland's economic underdevelopment, compared to England, had been the result of maltreatment of Ireland under the Union – in particular Ireland's inability to run an independent commercial and trade policy. Protectionism – building up industries behind tariffs and other trade barriers – was a major plank of Sinn Féin thinking during the struggle for independence, and once he came to power in 1932, de Valera had welded the country to this approach. The all-pervasive creed was that Ireland would be self-sufficient, and that we should reduce our dependence on the UK – a policy typified by the famous, oft-repeated expression: 'We should burn everything British except their coal.' This resulted in our being relatively isolated from the rest of Europe and the world. Ireland's insularity was, I believe, compounded by the experience of the Second World War, when countries that were not directly involved in the war remained isolated from major global changes.

By the late 1950s, this economic strategy was clearly failing, but it was still strongly associated with de Valera, who still commanded huge respect among Irish people. To depart from the orthodoxy would have required great political courage, as well as economic insight and diplomatic skill.

So this young man was appointed secretary general of the most important government department, the Department of Finance, and wrote the blueprint for how Ireland was to get out of the quagmire. The new strategy was, in essence, that Ireland had to open up economically to the rest of the world; this meant abandoning the policy of protectionism that de Valera had pursued with such single-mindedness for so long. We had to trade with the world and attract foreign industry. (It is hard to believe now, but in the 1930s, Fianna Fáil had introduced legislation to *prevent* foreign investment in Irish industries.) *Economic Development* laid the foundation for the economic growth that took place in Ireland in the 1960s and beyond.

In the period that followed, Ireland pursued a strategy of looking outwards rather than inwards. The Industrial Development Agency (now IDA-Ireland) began to bring in overseas multinationals, to set up manufacturing bases here, and to industrialise the country. At the time, the Irish economy was predominantly agricultural; there had been no Industrial Revolution, such as had occurred in Britain, and indeed in Northern Ireland, in the nineteenth century. After *Economic Development,* the slow process of industrialisation began, and by the early 1970s, people were beginning to return to Ireland: some of the people who had emigrated in the 1950s came back and started to work in manufacturing industries in particular.

This economic shift was to give rise to a new openness and outward-looking approach across Irish life. In the early 1960s, for example, the first tentative approach was made to join the Common Market – an application that was blocked by Charles de Gaulle, who did not want Britain to join. Of course, we became full members in 1973. There was a more general opening up in our culture, driven in part by the advent of television in the 1960s, and there was the first inkling of a new approach to Northern Ireland, with the Lemass–O'Neill talks – which, sadly, failed to avert the descent into the abyss in the 1970s. Later, we saw major social changes, such as equal pay and challenges to restrictions on contraception, and on divorce. These were all part of an opening up of Irish society that began with Whitaker's shift in economic thinking.

One of the most important aspects of these changes was the educational revolution of the 1960s. At the time, it was argued that a more educated workforce was essential in order to make Ireland a more industrialised country, but, of course, education liberates much more than productivity: the education revolution was to profoundly change Irish society. For example, it led to far more career opportunities coming to depend on educational qualifications and individual merit, rather than family inheritance.

The Labour Party can claim much credit for this revolution, which was eventually led by the Fianna Fáil Minister for Education, Donagh O'Malley. A couple of years ago, I was contacted by a postgraduate student who was looking for a copy of the Labour Party's 1962 education policy. Barry Desmond keeps a copy of everything, so I contacted him. Sure enough, he produced a copy of the policy: in fact, it was he, along with the former Supreme Court Judge

Catherine McGuinness – who was then on the Labour Party's education committee – who wrote it. They produced a fabulous document which included many of the proposals that were later adopted by O'Malley.

The paper advocated establishing the regional technical colleges, and mooted free secondary education and student grants, or student support of some kind. These policies were then incorporated into the party's manifesto for the 1965 general election. After that election, O'Malley lifted the policy, lock stock and barrel, and started to implement it. As in so many other fields, Labour was at the forefront of thinking as Ireland modernised.

One thing that interests me most about this period, beginning with Whitaker's report, was the role of Seán Lemass in driving the change politically. While Whitaker was the young, innovative civil servant, Lemass was a Fianna Fáil stalwart, who had been central both to the founding of the party in the 1920s, and to the development of the policy of protectionism in the 1930s. He had, after all, served for many years as Minister for Industry and Commerce. For Lemass, as Taoiseach, to endorse and support the changes that Whitaker was prescribing, required a willingness to challenge long-standing orthodoxies with which he was himself associated.

Historians will no doubt argue over who was driving whom. Was it the political leader who was urging on the civil servant, or the other way round? Whitaker, I suspect, was more fiscally conservative than Lemass, arguing in *Economic Development* that government investment in social infrastructure like schools and hospitals had to be curtailed in order to finance economic investment. In the event, the total level of state investment increased by a lot more than had been envisaged in the original strategy. Was this the influence of Lemass?

Looking back, Lemass himself does not strike one as the most charismatic of figures. However, I greatly admire him, and what he achieved. This is despite the fact that it was his skill as a political organiser, and his understanding of working people, that was in many ways responsible for building up Fianna Fáil in the 1920s and 1930s – at Labour's expense! Our traditional status as the 'half-party' in a two-and-a-half-party system, in contrast to other European countries, where social-democratic parties have flourished, owes much to Lemass's efforts on behalf of Fianna Fáil at that time. Many people who in other countries would have been natural Labour supporters became committed Fianna Fáil voters. We have to remember, however, that Lemass's Fianna Fáil was a very different party from the Fianna Fáil we know today. Although the party was socially conservative in many ways, it was not then the political vehicle for Thatcherite thinking and political insider-ism that it is now. Instead, it supported state-led investment, and social programmes, particularly in housing. For people like my mother and my stepfather, who were lifelong Fianna Fáil members, Fianna Fáil represented working people and small farmers like themselves.

I got to know T. K. Whitaker when I was appointed minister of state at the Department of the Marine in the rainbow coalition government of 1994–97. At the time of my appointment, a number of controversies, relating to inland fisheries and fish farming, were raging. It was shortly after what was known as the rod-licence dispute. There was also a growing debate about the collapse in wild sea trout stocks in the west, particularly in Mayo and Galway. This collapse was attributed to fish farming – specifically salmon farming – which was taking place in a number of the estuaries. It was believed that lice from the fish farms were attacking the wild stock.

The secretary general of the department advised me that the person I needed to meet to discuss all these issues was none other than Dr Whitaker. Whitaker is a passionate salmon angler: he is from Down but has fished in Mayo all his life. His autobiographical volume *Interests*, published in 1983, contains chapters on 'Financial Turning Points', but also on 'My First Salmon'! He had been appointed chairman of various working groups which had been set up to investigate the problem of declining sea-trout stocks. Whitaker was spoken of with great respect: in my time in government, I was struck by how greatly he was admired by civil servants.

Of course, I knew of Whitaker's reputation, and had heard and seen the lectures and interviews he had given on radio and television. Now I found myself sitting across the table from him as he explained what was happening to fish stocks, and why. While this was far removed from the great issues of economic policy of the 1950s and 1960s, I could immediately see why he was seen as embodying so much that is good in the Irish public service.

He was very gentle and soft-spoken, and very respectful of elected representatives. He offered his opinions but did not try to tell me what to do. Instead, his approach was to say 'These are your options' and 'This is what you might consider', and then to act as a sounding board. In a way, he was a classic civil servant. It was a case of: 'You are the minister, and you are the one who decides, but you are going to decide based on sound information and advice.' I found him incredibly impressive; he had a great command of all the topics on which he offered opinions.

I met Whitaker several times after that and came to appreciate his personal passion for wild salmon and for its conservation, and for what effective conservation entailed. He was very clear-sighted. For my part, in my capacity as minister of state, I became fascinated by the story of the salmon and its incredible journey; the abiding wonder in which Whitaker held this creature certainly motivated me. I was persuaded that we had to act to conserve wild salmon. We didn't go as far as Whitaker would have liked, however: he wanted me to ban drift netting, but at that time this wasn't feasible. Instead, we greatly restricted the practice by limiting it to daylight hours and reducing the duration of the fishing season. We also brought in several measures which were aimed at enhancing stocks.

Were we to pick up a newspaper today, we would be repeatedly presented with the names of the supposed movers and shakers in this country: the people written about in celebrity and social columns, including business people, sports stars, media figures and entertainers of one kind or another. At the same time, we are invited to dislike public servants and to accept a caricature view of the public service: that it is a great, bloated bureaucracy full of grey, unenterprising gnomes, which hold the rest of us back. In contrast, Whitaker stands out as an example of a public servant who was enormously enterprising and who had an immense impact on the life of the country. He was innovative and far-sighted – prepared to jettison a set of ideas that didn't work, but keenly aware of the dividing lines that are necessary in a well-functioning democracy. He is also unusual in that his role has been widely known and publicly acknowledged, in a public service which traditionally shrinks from publicity, both for the service itself and on the part of the individuals who work in it.

Whitaker represents a fine tradition among Irish public servants. Whereas the public-service ethos was once respected and valued, in recent years debate and discussion about it has taken on an almost exclusively negative tone. This was brought home to me on one occasion when the boom was at its height, when a friend of mine told me about a job he'd applied for – quite a senior job – in the public service. He had experience in the private sector, and had run his own business. One of the questions he was asked before the interview was: 'Why are you applying for a job like this? Why aren't you out there making money?' The attitude seemed to be that success could be measured only by how much money you were making, and that the public service must therefore be a place for underachievers.

I am firmly convinced that the public service needs major reform but that, in order to achieve real reform, we have to start from the proposition that public services matter, and that there is such thing as a public-service ethos. This ethos is different from what (quite properly) drives the private sector – not better or worse, but different.

The public system is full of people of talent and commitment; the key challenge is how to unlock these people's energy. One of the great failures of the last decade and a half has been Fianna Fáil's unwillingness to modernise the public service. Despite all the initiatives and buzzwords, progress has been minimal, and there are areas where the capacity of the system has been eroded.

One problem, for example, has been the decline in the role played by professionals within the public service. Something I saw happening in the local authority service, was the change in the way in which public work was carried out. Previously, county engineers designed the roads and the sewage schemes, and the county architects designed the housing schemes. We then moved from having that kind of 'in house' professional experience, drawing from a pool of public-service professionals, to a situation where we had fewer and fewer of them, and more work was contracted out to consultants.

And where are our public-service economists? Every time an economic report is required, the government sends for a firm of accountants. The increased use of consultants has undermined the development of in-house skills and expertise within the civil service. I doubt very much that a public servant would nowadays be given the remit to do what Dr Whitaker did back in the late 1950s.

Another worrying feature of recent decades has been the way in which our civil service has become politicised, with one party in office more than any other. Fianna Fáil have used the public service as a political pawn, such as in their botched decentralisation plan – an idea that had a lot of merit but was handled very badly. Public servants were treated as if they were cattle, who could be shipped off to 'Parlon Country'. It was vulgar.

Today, when it comes to presenting its case to the public, the civil service is stuck in a sort of no-man's-land. It was always part of our political tradition that the government would speak for the civil service, and that it, in turn, would remain largely anonymous: the civil service would stay in the background, and when it was attacked, the minister would come out and defend it and explain what they are doing. In fact, legally, ministers are accountable for their departments. In recent times, however, it has very often been the case that the government has led the attacks on the public service.

Of course, it never made sense that a minister should technically be responsible for every last paper clip in their department, or for the actions of every single official. But as things stand, no one can be held accountable for failures in government. In so far as there is any structure of accountability left, everyone in the department is responsible for everything, and no one is *actually* responsible for anything. It doesn't work. What we need instead is a new structure, whereby each department sets out who is responsible for what, and whereby the relevant minister is responsible, not for matters over which they cannot reasonably be expected to have any control, but for the decisions they made, or didn't make, once they became aware of a particular problem.

Up to now, the debate on the public service has been framed by those who have an ideological, or in some cases a commercial, agenda. Many are hostile to the idea of public service in the first place, and would privatise much of it if they had their way, because that is their view of the world. You also have to ask yourself, whether all proposals for privatisation are made in the public interest, or to serve the private interests of those who stand to get a 'slice of the action'.

Who is responding for the public service? Largely it has been trade unions, but trade unions cannot respond effectively for the public service because they have a particular role to play, which is largely focused on pay and working conditions, and they will inevitably be defensive. There has been nobody saying: 'Well, actually this is what we do; these are the services we provide.' Traditionally, that is the responsibility of government, but Fianna Fáil abandoned this when they discovered that it was more popular to attack the public service.

The public service *does* need to be reformed, and it *is* possible to produce meaningful reform. But public-service reform will be brought about only by people who believe in public services in the first place. Reform has to result in better value for money, but cost savings cannot be the starting point, or the sole focus, of reform; otherwise, we will get the sort of crude cuts that have been recommended in the McCarthy report.

Instead, we have to start from the point of view of the consumer, the client, the customer – in the end, the public. How do we achieve a better quality of public service? By public service I am talking about everything, whether it is health, education or social welfare. The starting point is the service. If we believe in public provision of certain things, and in effective regulation, then we have to hire the best people we can find to provide these services.

The vast majority of public servants are hard-working people who are committed to doing their job within the public-service remit. Yes, of course there are some who are not pulling their weight or are not up to the job – as you will have in any workplace. This cannot be ignored. But we also have to motivate people. For reform to succeed, we have to work with the staff themselves, who after all know the system best, and make them part of the change, rather than taking a casual and off-hand approach to them, as has been the case up to now.

A major issue we have to address is the culture of avoiding mistakes rather than taking risks; this is directly related to how we, as a society, react when something goes wrong. If we look at the way in which problems in the public service are treated in the media, we don't seem to allow for any exercise of judgement. Our test is: 'What went wrong? Where's the paperwork?' And the paperwork then becomes the most important aspect: having the 'boxes ticked' becomes more important than using good judgement. We need to move our way of governing from 'box-ticking' to using judgement and taking measured risks. We have to shift the focus away from whether or not someone made a mistake, or whether or not something went wrong, to whether the best decision was made at the time, and for the right reasons. We must encourage people who work in the public service to think laterally and in a joined-up, multifaceted way. Again, we can look to Dr Whitaker as an example.

Basing reform on the needs of citizens means having an eye to detail, and having a joined-up approach to government. One of my biggest bugbears as a constituency TD, for example, is means-testing. Take, for example, somebody who loses their job and applies for a social welfare payment. First, they are means-tested by the Department of Social Protection. While they're waiting for the social welfare payment, they may have to apply to the community welfare office for a supplementary payment to tide them over, and they are means-tested again for that – this time by the Health Service Executive. They then apply for a medical card, and another means test is carried out, this time by a different section of the HSE. They apply for a local authority house, and the local authority means-tests them. If one of the children is going to third level and they apply for a grant, they're means-tested again – by a different section of the same local authority. The same information is required for each means test, and each time they have to go back to the social welfare office to get the thing stamped. If they apply for secondary benefits, like rent allowance or the back-to-school allowance, they are means-tested again. It's lunacy! Why not use the first means test for all relevant applications, and have a simple 'change of circumstances' adjustment if required? It would be less humiliating for the individual, and more efficient and cost-effective to administer.

The same inability to take a joined-up approach to government explains some of the worst failures of the boom years. Why did we not make more progress on dealing with poverty during the boom? The problem is that, at its heart, poverty in Ireland is not a money issue. Of course, income is a factor, but poverty is also down to education, housing and infrastructure, to name but a few of its dimensions. Spending in these areas did increase during the boom, but we did not bring together the different arms of government in a way that could make a meaningful impact on the problem.

That is why one of most interesting projects in Ireland today is 'youngballymun' – an initiative that is jointly funded by a charity and the state. The idea behind the project is simple, but potentially very powerful. It uses a small amount of money, to reorganise, refocus and re-energise the various state services for children that are provided in Ballymun, in order to coordinate and deliver those services more effectively. This includes bringing in leading international experts to work with the professionals in the area, and to rethink the way in which services are provided. With better coordination and fresh thinking, there are many areas where we can make a far greater impact with the money that is already being spent.

We need to reform our public service, but we also need to defend it. The Labour Party believes in public services, and we say: there is a public space, and there is a public ground. There are things that we have to provide in common, and we provide them in common by paying our contribution into a pool, through taxation. We should contribute according to how well off we are. That is what fairness requires: the better off we are, the more we put into the pot. And if the day should come when we're in trouble or we hit hard times, it is expected that we'll have a safety net we can use.

For me, one lesson from the recession is an increased awareness that we need each other. During the boom, we lost sight somewhat of those connections we have with each other – how we ultimately depend on each other. We lost sight too of a kind of patriotism: the practical patriotism of service – to the community, to the state, and to each other. We cannot neglect it in good times, because we will really need it when times are bad.

True patriotism means a lot more than wearing a funny hat on St Patrick's Day. Even in the United States, one of the most free-market countries in the world, patriotism and service are seen as one and the same, and service is honoured, valued and appreciated. We lost sight of that truth in the frenzy of the property bubble. Now we have to find it again.

The concept of serving the public must be put back centre-stage, whether it is somebody following a career, a person becoming involved in the political or civic life of the country, or an individual doing voluntary work, as so many people do. This ranges from the people we see on a Saturday morning picking up litter and putting the flowers on the roundabout for the Tidy Towns committee, to the people who train football teams and run dance classes – all the things that people do that make up the fabric of society. This is all about serving the public, and you cannot have a society without it.

We need to have the modern-day Dr Whitakers running our government departments – the very best people running these important arms of the state to deliver outstanding public service – and we have to have a drive for excellence in the public service. We need to get back to the idea that there are jobs and roles and organisations where the governing idea is service to the public, and that people can be motivated by that goal. However, we need to remember that service cannot be confined to full-time public servants. It is a duty and a privilege for all of us, and part of what it means to be a citizen.

10
Matt Byrne

Matt Byrne was the person who convinced me that the environment was a working-class issue. It was the late 1980s, and we had been talking in my house in Shankill about various issues relating to the environment, as we often did. The view among some on the left at the time was that concern about the environment was a luxury that only the better-off could afford. The greatest challenge was jobs. You had a stark choice: you could industrialise, or you could protect the environment. Matt didn't buy it. He refused to accept an argument that put economic rights and environmental justice in opposing camps. Instead, he took the view that the two were related: well-off people always have the means to improve their environment, or escape it, while those in more straitened circumstances have to live with the environment they have, however damaged, polluted, dangerous or depressed it might be.

I became friendly with Matt Byrne, whom I met shortly after I was elected to Dun Laoghaire borough council in 1985, through my work as a local councillor. Matt was a very jolly man with a bubbly personality. He was an enthusiast – about what he did for a living, and all the issues which engaged him. He worked as a bricklayer for the Office of Public Works, based in the depot on Lad Lane. He was passionate about heritage and the environment, a staunch man of the Left, and an active member of An Taisce. I too was interested in the environment, but it was my friendship with Matt, and his infectious enthusiasm for the subject, that turned my interest into a lifelong commitment.

Soon after I was elected to the council, Matt and I became involved in a campaign in Dun Laoghaire called Harbour Watch. There was a proposal to build a private marina in the old coal harbour in Dun Laoghaire, and Matt, myself and others, including Dr John de Courcy Ireland, Labour councillor Jane Dillon Byrne, Charlie Pearson, Jack O'Sullivan, John O'Sullivan, Cecily Golden and Noel Brien came together and set up the Harbour Watch committee to fight the proposal. We met on Friday nights in Matt Byrne's house on Tivoli Terrace, and were united in a passionate belief that Dun Laoghaire Harbour should remain a public amenity, and not go into private ownership.

In early March 1988, the plans for the marina were revealed. The coal harbour – which is so called because it was close to where the old coal boats docked – is near the West Pier. At that stage, Dun Laoghaire did not have its own harbour company or harbour authority, and came under the control of the OPW, and later the Department of the Marine. The plans were for a massive marina, with hundreds of yacht moorings, apartments, shops, a hotel and conference centre, indoor tennis courts, restaurants, bars and other kinds of leisure facilities. All of this – every single amenity – was to be in private hands. We were horrified by the proposal. Some of the people who were promoting it were close to one Charles J. Haughey, and both he and the Fianna Fáil minority government approved of the plan. The people of Dun Laoghaire objected to the proposals, but, then, they had seen it all before: there has been a constant battle over the years to retain Dun Laoghaire harbour and seafront as a public amenity. That March, our ad hoc committee was formed, and the campaign was developed. There was strong local opposition to the proposals, and eventually, as a result of considerable pressure, the government set up a 'departmental committee' to review the plan. Ultimately, the development was shelved.

John de Courcy Ireland, the chairperson of the Harbour Watch committee, had been keenly involved in left-wing causes throughout his life. My friendship with John developed during the campaign, and influenced me greatly. John de Courcy Ireland was the leading maritime historian of our time, and probably this country's first serious environmentalist, certainly in the public eye. He was a remarkable man who was recognised far more abroad than he was here.

I was a regular caller to John's house in Dalkey, on Sorrento Terrace – which has been described as Dublin's Amalfi coast. There was an old bell – the kind you jangle – and either John or his wife Betty would open the door. Entering their house was like walking into a living library: there were piles of newspapers and paper clippings everywhere. John was an incredibly prolific letter-writer: I received letters from him regularly, even though we would see each other very often. All his letters were written in longhand, and he had a huge file of copies of them. Ever the conservationist, he would use every scrap of paper, writing out to the edge of the page. He was deeply involved in the Maritime Institute, which was in charge of the Maritime Museum in Dun Laoghaire, and was secretary of the RNLI for many years.

In fact, John nominated me as a candidate when I was first elected to the Dáil, in 1989. I have a photograph of us at the county sheriff's office on Arran Quay, me with my mop of red hair, handing in my papers and the deposit. Papers safely lodged, John turned to me and said that the last time he had nominated a candidate for the Dáil was in 1943, and that that candidate was Jim Larkin! It's a little living link in history of which I am very proud; the broadcaster Tom McSweeney made reference to it at John's funeral ceremony in Monkstown Church.

It was from John de Courcy Ireland that I learned my appreciation for the sea: its historical value in terms of travel and fishing, the importance of shipping for an island state, and the need to have good ports and a good marine infrastructure. The cloud of volcanic ash, which so disrupted European transport links in 2010, has highlighted how important it is for us to maintain a reliable surface link with the rest of Europe. John was one of the first people to talk to me about the depletion in our fish stocks, and the important role of fish farming if we were both to feed the world's growing population,

and to ensure that we do not wipe out whole species. The appreciation and knowledge of the sea which I gained from John would
prove extremely useful when I became Minister of State for the
Marine in 1994.

One of the first things I set out to do as Minister of State was to
draw on the wealth of knowledge that we have as an island nation:
I arranged a number of public consultations around the country to
develop a national maritime policy. Ireland's coastline is longer than
that of France, yet, relative to its importance, it has received propor-
tionately little attention. We drew together fishermen, people who
worked in ports, those with a stake in the sea because of the industry
they worked in or through their involvement in tourism, and people
who simply had an interest in maritime policy and history. Everyone
had an opportunity to share their views; the exercise proved
extremely useful. The true value of the sea as a natural resource is,
however, still underappreciated. During my period as minister, the
rainbow coalition introduced laws against dumping at sea. Up to
then, it was perfectly legal for ships to use the seas around Ireland as
a sewage dump! While the quality of our water and our beaches has
improved since then, we can still do more to harness the full benefits
of the sea, which is probably our greatest natural resource.

What Matt Byrne and other inspiring environmentalists I have
met over the years have in common is their progressive approach to
the environment as a place for people – a place for living, for working, and for leisure. It is not something to be preserved in aspic,
behind high fences, whose protection is an end in itself. Matt

refused to accept what he saw as a false choice between social progress and a healthy environment. Rather, careful stewarding of the environment – the natural world, as well as public amenities like Dun Laoghaire seafront – is a key element of social progress. It's all about sustainability.

Like Matt, I cannot accept an argument for the environment that completely ignores the practical needs of people, any more than I could accept a view that what are sold as unquestionable economic imperatives can trample roughshod over environmental concerns. We should never accept the way such black-and-white arguments are presented and simplified, and should refuse to be forced into false choices that do not reflect the true complexity of many genuinely important issues. And like Matt, I believe that the environment *is* a left-wing issue. I believed that in the 1980s, when many people with otherwise similar political views as myself regarded it as being a bit marginal. Looking at the effects of the disastrous construction boom, fuelled by Fianna Fáil and their big-developer friends, on our environment, our quality of life, and our longer-term security, I believe it even more passionately now.

In the 1990s, Ireland did need more houses for its young and growing population, and the tens of thousands of Irish emigrants, cast out by the economic disasters of the 1980s, who were returning home to an economy that was creating up to a thousand jobs a week. Yet by 2005, the average price of a home was nine times the average industrial wage – putting home ownership far beyond the means of most single people, even those in decently paid jobs.

Instead of leading to the construction of houses in and near towns and cities, where people worked, speculation raised the price of building land to new heights, and pushed new housing estates further and further into the countryside, transforming once-small villages into satellite suburbs of Dublin or Galway or Cork, and putting enormous pressure on local infrastructure like roads, sewage systems, schools and flood plains. Now we had hundreds of thousands of young families on the move – from house to crèche, from crèche to school, from school to work, and back again – and faced with the same long commute the next morning. Car ownership jumped from 310 per 1,000 people in 1997 to 420 per 1,000 less than ten years years later. Since 1990, our carbon emissions from transport alone have increased by 176 percent.

Greed, speculation and the blind eye turned by both the Fianna Fáil–PD government, and local authorities anxious to bring in development levies, has left our towns and cities more closely resembling sprawling American suburbs than the attractive cities of our European neighbours. Cities like Dublin and Galway have spawned large, meandering suburbs, many lacking proper public transport and community infrastructure. This laissez-faire attitude to planning means that, although a wonderful new road can get you from Dublin to Galway in two hours, it might then take you an hour and a half, in gridlocked traffic, to get from one side of Galway city to the other!

The built environment – the quality of our cities, towns and villages – has a direct impact on our quality of life. That is what Matt meant when he said that some people can escape their surroundings and others cannot. Good planning is the difference between building a community, and just building houses. It can exacerbate, or it can lessen, the isolation felt by a parent caring for a small child at home. It determines how long you spend in your car, whether children can walk safely to school, and what teenagers do in their spare time. It is the difference between a thriving town centre, with good local employment, and one where business moves further and further out of the town, 'hollowing out' the centre.

The financial consequences of our recent property bubble are all too familiar, measured by both our ballooning national debt and our massive private mortgage debt. However, as the price of fossil fuels rises, the environmental consequences of our housing boom will grow in the longer term. Firstly, despite the fact that a third of our total housing stock is almost brand new, Irish homes are not very energy-efficient. It is easy to see why: Fianna Fáil delayed the introduction of higher insulation standards until 2003, and even then there was considerable scope for improvement. This means that, unless we undertake a major insulation programme, the cost of heating and lighting our homes will continue to go up. The second problem is where those houses are located. Haphazard planning has lengthened commutes, and made people far more dependent on having access to a car. However, the further houses are spread out from each other, the more expensive they are to serve with public transport. As the cost of petrol rises, the cost of commuting by car will increase too. On top of this, Ireland will be obliged to reduce its greenhouse-gas emissions significantly over the coming years – or pay substantial fines.

I am often struck by how energy-intensive our lives have become in the space of just one generation. For years growing up in Caltra, we didn't have a fridge. That wouldn't have been unusual in rural Ireland in the 1960s. Now, for many families, multiple televisions, larger homes, and two cars are the norm. If the rest of the world used energy as we do in Europe, we would need three planets; if the rest of the world used energy like the United States, we would need five. Global warming is nature's stark message that this kind of level of consumption is not sustainable. Nor are the consequences far off in the future. On holiday in Canada a few years ago, my family and I visited the Athabasca Glacier. Standing at the foot of it, you could see a marker showing that the glacier had retreated by 1.5 kilometres in just 125 years. Of course, global warming is not just about melting ice in the Arctic; it is about more extreme and erratic weather at home and abroad too.

The twin challenges of reducing our dependence on imported fossil fuels, and cutting our carbon emissions, will define the coming decades, in Ireland and beyond. Scientists estimate that 'peak oil' – the point after which oil stocks are in permanent decline and oil prices rise dramatically – may occur as early as 2030, or even before. Ireland spends €6 billion a year importing fossil fuels, making us especially vulnerable to fuel scarcity – and soaring fuel costs. While most focus of public debate is, understandably, on our immediate fiscal crisis, we have to avoid the nightmare scenario that would see Ireland emerge from this global financial crisis, only to walk straight into an energy crisis.

Talk of a 'green economy' as though it were separate from our actual economy makes no sense. The *only* sustainable recovery from today's acute economic crisis is one that steadily reduces both our dependence on expensive fossil fuels, and our carbon emissions. We need to take a longer-term view of our economic recovery. It is not enough just to get through the next five years, or the next political cycle. We have to ensure that there are jobs in a sustainable, competitive Irish economy for the next fifteen or twenty years, and beyond. As I see it, there are three conditions we have to fulfil to ensure that our economy is sustainable in the medium to longer term.

The first, and most cost-effective, is reducing how much energy we use in the first place. That means insulating homes and businesses to bring down energy bills, using new technologies like smart meters to reduce our electricity consumption, engineering a significant switch to public transport, and looking at new ways of heating our homes. For every €100 million by which we manage to reduce our €6 billion fuel bill, we will have €100 million more circulating in our economy, instead of that of Russia or Saudi Arabia.

The second is developing alternative sources of energy so that we have stable, affordable energy prices that businesses can count on. Fortunately, Ireland has abundant sources of renewable energy, including solar energy, biomass (such as biofuel crops), geothermal energy (generated from below the earth's surface), and in particular wind and ocean energy. In fact, Ireland has one of the richest wind and wave regimes in Europe.

Finally, we have to be ready to exploit these two necessities –

weaning ourselves off fossil fuels, and reducing our carbon footprint – to create new ideas and products that we can sell abroad, and to develop new services and new jobs. Ireland is not the only country facing these enormous challenges. The market for energy-efficiency products and renewable energy is a global one, and is growing apace. The race is on to develop technology – for example, in wave energy – that could be used all over the world. The economic value of these ideas – or intellectual property – is enormous. We need to be strategic in how we compete in this race – for example, combining our natural advantages in IT expertise and renewable energy to become a test bed for new technologies, which we can then sell to the rest of the world.

Future-proofing our economy is not confined to obvious areas like energy security. We also have to look at another area where we have an existing indigenous industry: food production. In 1980, the world's population was almost 4.5 billion. Today it is almost 7 billion. In another thirty years, it will be nearly 9 billion. Food production – something which is overlooked in the rush to endorse the more technologically sophisticated elements of the 'smart economy' – will be increasingly important. As the volcanic-ash crisis illustrated, we cannot presume that we will always be able to fly in green beans from South Africa, or have strawberries in winter. It is important that we do not lose the ability to provide a varied diet for our own population. At the same time, it is vital that we develop Irish food exports to sell into new markets, such as India and China.

The potential for growth in agriculture and fisheries must, of course, be tempered by a respect for the planet's natural limits. Rapid population growth will place a real strain on the natural environment, acting as a driver of deforestation, overfishing and depleted soils. Fair global trade agreements, which encourage responsible farming, fishing and aquaculture, will be essential. After all, to be an environmentalist is, inevitably, to be an internationalist. The only way we can prevent the seas being overfished, or crops being poisoned by harsh chemicals, or our atmosphere becoming a dumping ground, is through cooperation.

The same is true when it comes to averting runaway global warming; although it will affect everyone, it will hit people living in the world's poorest countries first, and hardest. As a negotiating bloc representing 500 million people, the European Union has the economic, political and moral authority to definitively shape the international climate-change agreement that will replace the Kyoto Protocol after 2012. Ireland's interests will be best protected by being part of that bloc, but we should also use our proud tradition of solidarity with some of the world's poorest people to ensure that, whatever deal is reached, it is a fair one.

What I learned above all from Matt Byrne, John de Courcy Ireland, and other passionate environmentalists like them was the importance of taking a long-term view. Without it, we end up with a damaging property bubble and urban sprawl; the depletion, or even extinction, of our fish stocks; and unstoppable climate change that will destroy our grandchildren's natural inheritance. The environment is a place for *people*, not a museum piece. However, if the environment – whether the built environment of our towns and suburbs, or the natural world – is to be a place for people indefinitely, it has to be treated with respect – and in particular, respect for its limitations.

Matt Byrne died in 1995. I sometimes reflect on our chats over tea and chocolate biscuits in his sitting room on Tivoli Terrace, and I hear again his wise words about how connected everything is: the local heritage of Dun Laoghaire; the need for good planning and public transport; the links between where we live, how we live, and the impact we have on other people's lives, both locally and globally. We need more of his approach and philosophy now, when the future of the global environment has never looked more perilous.

11
Joe Connolly

There are moments which are destined to be etched on your memory forever: the 'Where were you when . . . ?' times. One of the great such moments in Irish sport, and particularly in Galway sport, was not on the playing field at all. It was on the Hogan Stand in Croke Park, on the first Sunday of September 1980. Galway had just beaten Limerick in the all-Ireland hurling final to become champions for the first time since 1923. Galway's captain, Joe Connolly, was receiving the Liam McCarthy Cup on behalf of his team when he delivered a speech that departed so far from the established script, was such a torrent of emotion and oratory, that no one who witnessed it would ever forget it. It remains probably the greatest sporting speech ever made in this country, and he made it largely in Irish, his own native language. People had become accustomed over the years to the winning captain giving a speech which would begin with the line '*Tá an-áthas orm an corn seo a ghlacadh* . . . ', followed by thanks to everybody who helped – the manager, the team, all the supporters and the county board – and it usually ended with three cheers for the losing team. Not for Joe Connolly: too much had been at stake. In a fabulous rush of eloquence and outpouring of emotion, he captured perfectly the mood of the county and the supporters. It was a cathartic moment: Galway's hour had come. The fifty-seven-year famine was over.

I was in Croke Park that Sunday, standing on Hill 16, and I remember the details very clearly. It was a dry, sunny day. Galway put the game away in the second half and won comfortably. Of course, the thing about hurling is that it's never over until the full-time whistle: many a reversal of fortune has been sparked by a last-minute score. But the final result that day was Galway 2–15, Limerick 3 –9, under coach Cyril Farrell. This was Galway's third all-Ireland final in six years. It was a free-scoring match, but there was no doubt that we deserved to win. Of course, it was extremely disappointing for Limerick, but there was also a sense that, at long last, Galway's moment had come. Emotion filled the stadium to the brim, the crowd erupting with joy as Connolly raised the cup. Joe seized the moment as though he had been waiting for it his whole life – as, in a way, he had:

> People of Galway, after fifty-seven years the all-Ireland title is back in Galway. . . . It's wonderful to be from Galway on a day like today. There are people back in Galway with wonder in their hearts, but also we must remember people in England, in America, and round the world, and maybe they are crying at this moment. . . . People of Galway, we love you!'

Pope John Paul II had visited Ireland the previous summer, and had celebrated a youth Mass at Ballybrit Racecourse in Galway. He ended his sermon with the declaration: 'Young people of Ireland, I love you.' Playing on this final rallying cry was a bit tongue-in-cheek, of course, but Connolly was also making it clear that the team had won the cup for the people of Galway – not just those at home, but also Galway's large diaspora.

Galway winning the all-Ireland in 1980 was a seminal moment in the county's history. It wasn't just that Galway had won, it was also the first time since 1923 that the Liam McCarthy Cup was crossing the Shannon. The joy and ecstasy of the win were intensified because of the pain and loss which had preceded that day. In the period from the early 1970s, the Galway hurling team had started to improve: Galway was in the all-Ireland final in 1975, but Kilkenny beat them (though Galway did win the league title that year). Galway reached the all-Ireland final again in 1979; they lost, once more, to Kilkenny. I was in Eyre Square for the homecoming that year, when then-captain Joe McDonagh promised the crowd that Galway's day would come again – and so it did. However, Galway had suffered in hurling. It was the only team in Connacht that played at the top level. Roscommon would come and go. Occasionally there would be a Connacht final of sorts between Galway and Roscommon, which usually ended with a cricket score, and Galway winning. Most years, there was no Connacht final: Galway would be the last county standing.

The problem for Galway was that, down through the decades,

the Munster and Leinster championships were dominated by Cork, Kilkenny and Tipperary. Galway would then play one of the winning teams in the all-Ireland semi-final, usually winning or losing by a very small margin. We would arrive at the final, only to be beaten – again – by a small margin. We were the perpetual bridesmaid; unless we got to play more matches at this level, we always would be. Then, in the early 1960s, an attempt was made to rectify this handicap, by allowing Galway to compete in the Munster hurling championship. However, in their ten years in the Munster championship, they only ever won one match, against Clare in 1961. Off they went again, back up to reign supreme (if alone) in Connacht. As the 1970s progressed, it seemed that the potential was growing in the underage teams; however, the Liam McCarthy Cup continued to elude us.

There are a number of reasons why that particular moment in Croke Park in 1980 was so important for Galway. We arrived there as a people sharing a great hunger – Joe Connolly recently described the county as being 'ravenous' for all-Ireland success. Galway won their famous three-in-a-row in football in 1964, 1965 and 1966, when I was a child; the members of that team were our boyhood heroes. However, while football was important, the great ambition was to win in hurling.

They used to say that Galway's failure to win an all-Ireland final in the long, barren years from 1923 was due to a curse. The story went that a parish priest from somewhere in the county was piqued when some hurlers left his Mass early to play in a match in Dublin.

Incensed at such disrespect – not to mention impiety – he told them that as long as there were men from that parish playing hurling in Galway, the county would never win. This myth was an indication, perhaps, of Galway's growing despair – although after fifty-seven years, people were beginning to believe it! However, in 1980 the duck was broken, and we were free at last from the curse!

The win in 1980 was also significant to me on a personal level, because I knew a lot of the players on the team. One of them was Joe Connolly himself, whom I had got to know in UCG. Joe McDonagh, a future president of the GAA, had served on the student union executive with me. Joe didn't play that day in 1980 – he was injured – though many will remember him singing 'The West's Awake' at the end, his heart bursting with emotion. Father Iggy Clarke (who also didn't play that day due to injury) was in school with me in Garbally, as was Sean Silke. Consequently, while that victory in Croke Park in 1980 was an important event in Irish sporting history, from my individual perspective, it was a huge personal joy to see people whom I knew, and with whom I was friends, succeed in this thrilling sport, and walk up the steps of the Hogan Stand to receive their all-Ireland medals.

Even though we had been beaten year in, year out, Galway was, and is, a great hurling county. There are twenty senior hurling clubs in County Galway, where the game has its roots. Killimor, where my wife Carol is from, was where the first rules of hurling were written down, in the nineteenth century. Unfortunately for a county with a long hurling tradition, we do not have the all-Ireland records to show for it. No wonder that the win in 1980 reduced so many to tears! You can wait a long time for success, but it's worth it when you get there: when you reach the pinnacle, all the time spent climbing is forgotten. Just ask the Munster players who won the Heineken Cup in May 2006 after being runners-up twice!

Caltra is the football team of the parish where I grew up. In 2003, Caltra won the county final, and went on to win the all-Ireland final in Croke Park on St Patrick's Day 2004. As it happened, that particular period of success for the team coincided with a time in my life when I was spending a lot of time in Caltra. In the early 2000s, we were worried that my mother was becoming a little forgetful, a condition which was ultimately diagnosed as Alzheimer's. In 2002, my stepfather Tommy, who had been caring for her, had a car accident, and his own health declined. I began to spend more and more time in Caltra, caring for them both, and arranging for their care, most of which was provided by local women, particularly Margaret Carney.

It was a difficult time for us as a family, but was pure joy for Caltra. I brought my mother and Tommy to all Caltra's games in the club football championship. I remember one in particular: the all-Ireland club semi-final played in Markievicz Park in Sligo on a bitterly cold Sunday in February 2004. I put two overcoats on my mother and a big rug around Tommy, and fortified them both with a little whiskey I had decanted into a small water bottle at the last minute, before we left the house. I had anxious moments during the game, and wondered if I was guilty of some crime of negligence or irresponsibility as the Arctic wind whipped around us on the exposed stand!

As the final whistle blew in Croke Park on St Patrick's Day 2004, with Caltra having beaten the Kerry Gaeltacht by a single point, Joe Connolly's moment on the Hogan Stand came back to me. A few weeks later, there was a celebratory dinner in the Radisson Hotel in Galway. Tommy had played for the Caltra team which had last won a county title in 1943, and he was now one of its few surviving members. Those few elderly men were always the honoured guests at every event during that year; Tommy asked me if I would accompany him to the celebration in the Radisson.

By this stage, he was becoming quite infirm, and had occasional recourse to a wheelchair. As I wheeled him down the hotel corridor, towards the dining room, we met Joe Connolly coming towards us, in the company of Seán Purcell, the Galway football legend of the 1950s, who would have been an old hero of my stepfather's. Joe and I stopped to talk, to exchange a bit of banter. In the meantime, I noticed Tommy settling into deep conversation with Purcell, about the good old days of the 1940s and 1950s, when men were real men, and football was catch and kick!

That moment has stayed with me because it was the last time that my stepfather and I were out together socially, the last time we had a drink together. He died a few weeks later. Indeed, the great Seán Purcell also passed away within the year.

Every country needs its heroes, and every country looks to sport to produce them. Like so many people in Ireland, I love sport, and it takes up a considerable part of my leisure time. Coming from a part of the country where, both at club and county level, we've done very well, it's natural that I follow both hurling and football. I went to a school where we played rugby, and I have retained an interest in that too. Garbally College produced a significant number of successful international rugby players, including Ray McLoughlin, who captained the Ireland team through the mid-1960s and 1970s. Mick Molloy, second-row for Ireland in the 1960s, was a Garbally boy, as was the great Noel Mannion, and Ciaran Fitzgerald – probably our most famous gift to rugby. He was there in my time as a pupil. Ciaran Fitzgerald will forever be remembered for his famous injunction to the Ireland team the year they won the Triple Crown: 'Where's your f**king pride?' – a phrase that comes into my head occasionally when I'm at political meetings and the glass, for some, seems always to be half-empty!

I have a great interest in soccer, too. I do not support any team in particular, but I do follow the Premiership. One footballing personality whom I admire is Alex Ferguson. Since I became leader of a political party, I understand, better than ever, that you're only as good as your last match. It's hard to believe now, but Ferguson had real difficulties in his early days at Manchester United. He was not getting the results, and there was a lot of speculation about how long he would last. However, he stuck with it: he had a game plan, and it worked. He was, and is, extremely professional in his approach to the game, and demanded great discipline from his players. His focus means that he is the longest-serving manager in the English

Premiership – and, of course, he has remained loyal to the Labour movement.

Another is Paul McGrath, who grew up in the Tivoli Boys' Home in my constituency of Dun Laoghaire. Even after he had achieved considerable success abroad, Paul was always generous with his time, and would often come back to support the local clubs. There is enormous affection for him in the area, not least because he was a player from that golden period of Irish soccer, when we qualified for the European Championships in 1988 and beat England. There is no doubt in my mind that Italia '90 helped build the national self-confidence which helped to build the economic growth and success of the 1990s.

For such a small country, Ireland sustains a considerable variety of sports. As well as our indigenous games – hurling, Gaelic football, camogie, ladies' football and handball – we have a rugby team who are serious international contenders; a young soccer team that is showing potential; world-class golfers like Padraig Harrington and Rory McIlroy; boxing champions like Katie Taylor; and athletes like Derval O'Rourke – to name but a few. Our self-belief when it comes to international competitions, in whatever sport, is indefatigable: despite our size, our population, the variety of sports we play, and a scarcity of funding in many areas, if we make it to the international arena, we fully expect to win!

Our constant expectation of sporting excellence, given our size, should be an inspiration to us. As we grapple with the massive and difficult challenges that currently face our country – the economic crisis and the huge uncertainty about what lies ahead – we need to ask ourselves, what should our expectations be in other aspects of Irish life? We know that we are a hard-working people, and we understand that we can enjoy success disproportionate to the size of our population: just look at our global achievement in theatre, in film and literature, or the number of Irish people who occupy powerful positions in boardrooms all over the world. So why shouldn't we expect the same standards of success and achievement in our public life?

It is true that our sporting success has often come against the odds, but we can draw inspiration and hope from that too. The constant grind of bad news – the banking crisis, followed by the unemployment crisis, followed by the fiscal crisis – risks wearing us down. In these moments, we could do worse than to remind ourselves of Ciaran Fitzgerald's invocation: 'Where's your f**king pride?' We can overcome the odds. We can do it. We just need to believe – as we believe, against all odds, that Ireland will someday progress beyond the quarter-finals of the World Cup – that we are capable of succeeding in whatever we put our minds to.

Eventually, after fifty-seven years, the Liam McCarthy Cup did go to Galway – not Kilkenny, or Cork, or Tipperary. The glamorous day in Croke Park, when you raise the Liam McCarthy Cup and address the cheering crowd, is the punchline, not the whole story. Joe Connolly spent a lot of time running around wet fields in Castlegar to develop his skills and achieve the level of fitness that was necessary to succeed at that level. You could say that, as a country, we too have a long, hard road ahead of us, but, like any successful sportsperson knows, that hard road is the price you have to pay to achieve success. We have to fix our unemployment crisis, and our banking crisis, and our fiscal crisis, and we have to reinvent our economy and our democracy if we are to ensure that we never, ever find ourselves in this black hole again.

There is no such thing as overnight success. If we lay the foundations for a better Ireland now; if we face up to the challenge of a generation; if we make it a matter of pride that we *will* recover; and if we take both personal, and collective, responsibility for standing by our fellow Irishmen and women who have been most severely affected by this recession, and get people back into work; then we will, ultimately, reap the rewards. Our victory will be hard won – I am under no illusions about that – but, in the end, I am convinced of one thing: we will raise that cup.

12

Seán Ó Riada

My love of the Irish language and of Irish music stretches back to primary school, and to my two exceptional teachers, Michael Hogan and Mary Kilcommins. However, it was only when I rediscovered the language as an adult that I appreciated just how rich a store of culture, art and history it is. I came of age in the 1970s, when, largely due to the influence of the composer and broadcaster Seán Ó Riada, Irish music was experiencing a joyous renewal, stretching far beyond an Ireland which was languishing in the shadow of the Troubles, emigration, unemployment and increasingly bitter ideological battles.

Seán Ó Riada's legacy is the life he helped breathe into the Irish-language movement through his pioneering of a renaissance in Irish music. Born John Reidy on 1 August 1931, he went on to become not only one of Ireland's greatest composers, but also a director, an acclaimed performer, a well-loved broadcaster, and an influential lecturer in the school of music at University College Cork. Both of his parents were from farming backgrounds, and his father was a Garda sergeant. Like me, he attended secondary school with the help of a scholarship, and entered UCC in 1948 as a young student of music, Irish, Latin and Greek, also on a scholarship.

Ó Riada married Ruth Coughlan in 1953, but left Ireland for Paris two years later. He returned to Ireland as director of music at the Abbey Theatre, a post which he held until 1962, and which allowed him more time and freedom to compose. He composed scores for a number of films, but he is best known for his iconic orchestral score written for the 1959 film *Mise Éire*, which made him a national figure.

Ó Riada was instrumental in the renaissance of traditional Irish music, and the direction that it took from the 1960s onwards, when it moved out of a kind of *ceilí* formalism to a more expressive and exploratory style. He has been compared by Louis Marcus to James Joyce: both were artists who sought to revive the Irish artistic idiom through engagement with the world, and with other traditions. Both also sought freedom abroad, although, unlike Joyce, who opted for permanent exile, Ó Riada's response was an even deeper engagement with Irish culture, through its music and its language: he even went so far as to move his young family to Cúil Aodha in the West Cork Gaeltacht in 1963. Moreover, Ó Riada's fusion of the native with the international gave traditional Irish music a dynamism that chimed with Ireland's growing self-confidence at the time.

Ó Riada helped form the original Ceoltóirí Chualann, a revolutionary group of musicians for the period, which included many of the founder members of the Chieftains, one of the great traditional Irish groups. Ó Riada lived for a time in Galloping Green, near Stillorgan in south Dublin, where the Ceoltóirí Chualann would gather to rehearse. In fact, their name is derived from the Irish *cuala*, the old name for south county Dublin. As a young councillor in the area in the 1980s, I attempted to have a plaque put up on his old home.

Ultimately, Ó Riada's influence on the trajectory of Irish music is unquantifiable. We only have to look at of how far Irish music has travelled since the early 1960s, when it was regarded as something of a relic, to the Ceoltóirí Chualann, to the later Chieftains music, to collaborations with some of the great American musicians and folk singers. Even Bob Dylan cites the Clancy Brothers as a major influence on him!

This renaissance in Irish culture and identity was the backdrop to my childhood in the 1960s. I was part of a generation which came to adulthood at a time when the revival of Irish cultural nationalism – in both language and music – was to become tempered by disillusionment – with politics, and with the violent, sectarian turn taken by nationalism in Northern Ireland. This is a conflict which, I believe, has dogged Irish identity in the decades since.

I am not a native Irish speaker, and it is almost by chance that I had my primary education through Irish. I did not live in a Gaeltacht area: my family spoke English at home. Yet the principal of the small, two-teacher school to which my mother sent me had a boundless interest in Irish culture: all the business of the school day, even in the yard, was conducted through Irish. I also had a succession of good Irish teachers when I went to second level at Garbally, though it was an English-speaking school. But by the time I had finished my degree in University College Galway, I had almost entirely lost my ability to speak Irish. Firstly, I had stopped speaking the language at all; secondly, those who spoke Irish on campus did so only amongst themselves. If you weren't a native Irish speaker, and weren't from a Gaeltacht area, your Irish was somehow regarded as not being good enough. I didn't fit into the scene, and by the time I left university my Irish was almost gone.

However, while I was working in Galway as a branch secretary for the ITGWU, which represented workers in most of the factories in the Connemara Gaeltacht, my interest in, and use of, the language was renewed. These factories had made closed-shop agreements with the union, through Gaeltarra Éireann, the predecessor of Údarás na Gaeltachta. Closed-shop agreements are now largely a thing of the past, but in the 1970s it was normal practice for new companies to enter into an agreement with a trade union in which it was a condition of employment that every employee would join that particular union. This was to avoid having a multiplicity of unions in the same place of work: employers thought it better to have to deal with just the one. In the Gaeltacht, the Gaeltarra Éireann added a further condition: that the union would allocate a union official who could speak Irish and could conduct union business through the language. I found myself speaking Irish in factories in Connemara, in meetings with Gaeltarra Éireann, and even on Radio na Gaeltachta, in discussions about industrial disputes, tax marches or whatever the issue of the day was. The Irish which Michael Hogan had taught me was not buried too far beneath the surface, I discovered, and it began to come back.

Some things, however, were above the politics of language. There was a pay dispute in one of the factories I was serving, and I had gone there to conduct a meeting. Before the meeting started, the shop steward pulled me to one side and said that he and the section committee in the factory, all of whom were native Irish speakers, would prefer it if the meeting was conducted in English. I told them that, on the contrary, I was quite happy to do it in Irish. It wasn't unusual that meetings such as this one be conducted in English, because very often the employer might be from overseas: for example, there were Italians and British running subsidiaries of multinational companies located in the Gaeltacht. However, in this factory the employer was Irish, so there was no reason why the meeting couldn't be conducted in Irish. I asked him if he thought my Irish was not good enough. 'Oh, no, no', he said, 'you have very good Irish – but this is about money, and we don't want you to be making any mistakes!'

I certainly don't have perfect Irish, but even after leaving the Connemara factories long behind, I have managed to keep it up. I still often do interviews in Irish, partly as a spur to maintain it. I believe very strongly that knowledge of Irish opens up for us a rich seam of information about our own country: who we are and where we came from. When it comes to place-names, for example, a knowledge of Irish helps us understand where a particular name comes from, and this can tell us something about the fauna, the flora, the geography or the history of a particular area. Shankill, where I live, means 'the Old Church': there was originally an old church and an old cross in the area. A housing estate stands where the cross once was; the name of the village is the only clue that it was there. Leixlip is another place whose name peels back layers of history. Leixlip's name in Irish, Léim an Bhradáin, means 'the Leap of the Salmon'. *Lax* is also a Nordic word for 'salmon': the old Viking name for the settlement lives on in English. We can take any place-name and ask: what is this name whispering to us? The answer can tug a string that stretches back for more than a millennium. The Irish language translates who we are back to ourselves; if it disappeared, the loss would be incalculable.

Language experts who are monitoring the decline in minority and ethnic languages say that by 2100 the world will have lost more than half the seven thousand languages that are spoken today. That is, quite simply, a tragedy: a loss of knowledge that cannot be stored in any database. It is natural that languages evolve and, particularly given the transformation in communication brought about by the internet, that they do not stay within national borders. We are fortunate in Ireland to be an English-speaking country: in such an open economy as ours, this has worked to our advantage. However, it is perfectly possible to be a bilingual country, and to maintain that advantage. Yet there is a real risk that Irish as a spoken language will be irrevocably lost. We are, rightly, keen to conserve our heritage, and over the decades there have been a number of high-profile campaigns to save architectural monuments: like Wood Quay, or Dublin's Georgian houses, or the Hill of Tara. And yet, the greatest national monument, and our living heritage, is the Irish language. It is an ancient language that has survived invasions, colonisation, famine, emigration and wars, and it is therefore somewhat ironic that it is this generation – the most educated, most confident and, even still, the most affluent generation of Irish people yet – who may allow it to wither.

It is interesting that where there *has* been growth in the Irish language, it has largely been in urban centres. Better roads and communication infrastructure mean that the isolation that once made the Gaeltachts poor is now making them attractive locations for development. Consequently, Gaeltacht areas are being pushed further to the periphery. Driving west from Galway city, one now has to travel farther and farther before arriving at the Fíor Gaeltacht. When I was in university, Knocknacarra in Galway still had Irish-speaking people: one could argue that it was part of the 'real' Gaeltacht. Now, Knocknacarra is a suburb of the city like any other – although officially it is in the Gaeltacht.

In my view, there have been two major recent developments which have had a positive impact on the Irish language, its growth and retention. The first is Teilifís na Gaeilge, or TG4 as it is now known. This, of course, was established by Michael D. Higgins when he was Minister for the Arts and the Gaeltacht in the rainbow coalition. At the time, many regarded the station as, at best, a white elephant, and some sectors of the media were positively vicious in their antipathy towards it. However, it has since become a successful and well-regarded broadcaster. More importantly, it has also been successful in maintaining the sound of spoken Irish in the home – probably even more than Raidió na Gaeltachta, which is very much a Gaeltacht station, and which requires a conscious commitment on the part of the listener to tune in. The success of TG4 is that there is usually something on which will surprise the viewer, such as their sports coverage or one of their excellent documentaries. It is true that the Hollywood Westerns are in English, but it would be hard to dub John Wayne and make him sound like Mícheál Ó Muircheartaigh! In a way, this is another reason for TG4's approach-ability: it is not afraid to embrace English, and to acknowledge that its audience is not made up of monoglot Irish speakers.

The second positive development for the language is the growing number of Gaelscoileanna which have been established over the past decade. They have gained a foothold for the Irish language outside the Gaeltacht, in a diverse range of communities. I know there are those who criticise the Gaelscoileanna, saying that people only send their children to them because of their generally smaller pupil-to-teacher ratios, or because they are somehow 'more middle class'. I believe that this criticism is both inaccurate and unfair. Firstly, there are Gaelscoileanna serving a wide variety of communities, and children of different backgrounds; like their English-speaking counterparts, some Gaelscoileanna are designated disadvantaged schools. Secondly, the decision by parents, or sometimes pupils themselves, to be taught through Irish is one that requires considerable commitment. Learning through what is, for most children, a second language is a challenging task. The majority of children who attend Gaelscoileanna do not come from Irish-speaking homes, yet having a child being educated through Irish can spur a renewed interest in the language in the rest of the household. This is exactly the grassroots, bottom-up approach to cultivating an interest in Irish that has been so underdeveloped in Irish-language policy to date.

One of the most common arguments against continued state support for the Irish language is that public policy has failed to halt its decline as a spoken language. Indeed, the retention of the Irish language is probably the only public-policy objective that has been consistently observed, whatever government was in power, since the foundation of the state. One of the reasons why, despite such consistency, the objective of that policy has not been realised is that it is not just up to the state, or indeed a small minority of enthusiasts, to defend the importance of what is our shared, national heritage. I firmly believe that the maintenance of the Irish language needs to be a shared responsibility, to be addressed collectively.

Somewhere along the way, the Irish language became associated with conservatism – a weapon of a narrow, insular kind of nationalism that many people did not identify with. Once, the revival of the Irish language was a celebration of democracy and political independence, but as soon as Irish became the badge of 'Official Ireland', it became stultifying. This was not helped by the fact that the preservation of Irish became a platitude – an aspiration, like world peace, that politicians and others said they were in favour of, but did not actually believe was possible. Combined with the hypocrisy of the public *cúpla focal*, a mere nod in the direction of the language for appearances' sake, is it any wonder that whole generations of Irish people found themselves turned off the language? A passion for Irish became the preserve of a small, dedicated section of the population. Irish-language enthusiasts have not always done the cause a favour: they have at times been elitist or aggressive in their defence of the language. The key to the retention and growth of the Irish language is not an obsession with its preservation, but rather a concern with its popularisation. It has to be treated as a living thing, not a museum piece. Where the language has succeeded in becoming more popular is where it has been associated with enjoyment, music, contemporary culture, and change – Seán Ó Riada's opening up of Irish music being a case in point.

The revival in Irish music in the 1960s and 1970s shook off the baggage of 'official' nationalism, and embraced a new one, which was younger and less reverent. The Irish language benefited from this cultural shift, although it is worth pointing out that irreverence and subversion has always been part of the Irish language, as much as it has of the culture and the people – something that was suffocated by the anointing of Irish as the medium of a 'true' Ireland. Examples of this can be found in some of the great Irish writers, like Máirtín Ó Cadháin. Ó Cadháin was the James Joyce of Irish literature, and *Cré na Cille* is its *Ulysses*. Indeed, Ó Cadháin, Liam O'Flaherty, and Pádraic Ó Conaire were all writers who did not cleave to the prevailing orthodoxy. Ó Cadháin was a radical republican who was interned in the Curragh in the 1940s. O'Flaherty and Pádraic Ó Conaire were left-wingers, the latter canvassing for the Labour Party in Galway in the 1920s.

My favourite example of the tension between the irreverence and wit of the Irish language, and officialdom, comes from a hurling match in the late 1980s. A group of enthusiastic Galway supporters unfurled a banner urging their team to '*Scaoil amach an bobailín!*', or 'Let it rip!' – though the literal translation is a little more colourful! A GAA official confiscated the banner for the duration of the game, on the grounds that it was a political flag – although perhaps he just objected to the explicit phrasing! Needless to say, the steward ensured that the slang '*Scaoil amach an bobailín*' was to enter the popular lexicon, even becoming the name of an Irish-language programme on RTÉ: some things simply cannot be repressed.

Few issues excite more heated debate and polarised opinions than the place of the Irish language in contemporary Ireland. What those on either end of the spectrum sometimes miss is that pluralism – of language, religion and culture – is part of Ireland's history, from the Celts and the Vikings to the Normans and the Planters, and Catholics, Protestants and Dissenters. Pluralism will also be part of Ireland's future. We are an English-speaking country, in a world where English is the global language of popular culture and business – something which has the potential to crowd out other languages.

Maintaining and enriching the Irish language and the associated culture will require more innovative thinking on our part.

Irish is not widely spoken, not because of the way it is taught, but because there are so few opportunities for people to use what they learnt in school. It is not radical to propose making Irish a non-compulsory school subject, as some have, when it is what happens beyond the school gate that really matters! Rather, it is up to all of us, if we value the language at all, to use it. Who says that a Gaeltacht has to be on the western seaboard? There are more Irish speakers in Dublin, so could we not have a 'virtual Gaeltacht' in the capital? Local authorities anywhere in the country could promote everyday use of the language very easily, through libraries, but also through offering preferential rates for businesses which conduct their affairs through Irish. Local cafés and restaurants could have one or two days a week where staff and customers speak Irish together. People are often embarrassed to speak Irish, feeling that they have forgotten all they learned in school. But often it's not forgotten at all, just deeply buried: all we have to do is 'scaoil amach an bobailín'!

Pluralism goes both ways: Irish language and Irish culture is not a threat to diversity, just like the arrival of people from all over the world to live and work in Ireland over the past ten years has not destroyed Irish culture. We have reason neither to apologise nor to be defensive. We can value our Irish heritage while being open to the richness of other cultures, and to those who seek to share in ours.

For a long time, pride in our national identity took a battering.

Between the Troubles, and the IRA's campaign of violence in the name of Ireland, and the economic depression of the 1980s, which saw tens of thousands of people emigrate every year from a country that could not offer them a future, declaring one's Irishness was not without its difficulties. This is particularly true for the tens of thousands of Irish people who worked in Britain during the IRA's bombing campaign there. With the peace process in the 1990s, and the rapid economic growth of the Celtic Tiger, which attracted returning Irish emigrants, and then economic migrants from all over the world, came a growing self-confidence, and a renewed pride in being Irish.

For me, what it means to be Irish is a very personal thing. I love the Irish language – a language I learned, lost, then found again. I believe it is an invaluable key to our history and our heritage. But being Irish is not a creed or a colour, or even simply a fluency in our native language.

Being Irish is an outward-looking pride – one that locates Ireland as an active member of the European Union; that is proud of Ireland's solidarity with developing countries; that is proud of our contribution to music, literature, art and theatre; that is conscious of a diaspora which has made a contribution to the emigrants' host countries in the four corners of the globe. Notwithstanding the damage done to our international reputation recently, we still have many reasons to be proud and, crucially, to remain open to the world and all it offers.

Epilogue:
The Journey Ahead

This book has been written over a period of more than six months, in a series of moments snatched from the day-to-day demands of political life. As I come to finish it, and commit it to print, the economic crisis is becoming ever more acute. The national mood is increasingly dark. So what is the point of a book like this? What relevance does it have to the future?

As I said in the introduction, I think it is perfectly reasonable for people to want to know more about what makes someone who wishes to lead their country 'tick'. We can't know what decisions they are going to have to make in the years ahead, but we can get some insight into how they may approach those decisions. What has shaped them? Who has influenced them?

But there is something else important at work here as well. The deeper the crisis, the more people fall back on the question of what they truly believe, and what is *really* important to them. We have seen this during the years since the bubble burst. Several people have told me that the economic downturn has forced them to rethink what is really important in their lives; they have, in some cases, been surprised by the answer.

Writing this book has been a bit like that for me. It has brought to the surface issues and episodes that had faded into the background, and has given me an opportunity to reflect on what I think matters. As I write this, in the week after 'Black Thursday', the day when we finally came to know the full cost of the blanket banking guarantee, I know one thing for sure – that, as a country, values matter, now more than ever. What we think is important, who we think matters, how we see our future – these things will all be severely tested in the months and years ahead.

So, let me try to summarise what I have learned from writing this book in a short credo. Here goes. I believe . . .

I believe that Ireland is a great country. We have a beautiful island, a long and rich history, and above all, great people. My appreciation for this country began with the stories I learned from my grandmother, but it continues today in the people I have the privilege of meeting through my job – people from every conceivable walk of life. Whether it's a young entrepreneur who has come up with a new idea and turned it into a business, or a large multinational that is at the cutting edge of shaping the internet, or a person who is making a difference in their community, or someone who is just doing everything they can to get their family through the recession. The people I have written about in this book, most of whom I have known personally, are just examples of that. We may have a lousy government, but we have a great country.

We can, and we will, get through this crisis. As a trade union official in the 1980s, I saw the impact of the last big recession up close. I remember sitting in canteens with people who were losing their jobs, and who wondered if they would ever work again. In fact, they did, many of them working for themselves. We have to remember that there is always hope.

We will get through the crisis, but we will only get through it as One Ireland. Setting one group of people against another was never a good idea, and the time for that is past. We have to pull together if we are to pull through. And to do that, we have to have a vision of the future – of what we are trying to achieve. To me, that means coming together as One Ireland, and staying One Ireland afterwards. We are going to have to make hard decisions in the coming years, but they have to be the *right* hard decisions. We have to build a country where everyone can work to fulfil their potential

I also believe that change is possible. During the 1950s, Ireland drifted into a dark cloud of pessimism. But change happened. New thinking, much of it supplied by T. K. Whitaker, meant that a crisis was turned into an opportunity, and a whole new phase of our history was begun. I was the direct beneficiary of that, being the first person in my family ever to go into third-level education, but I was only one of many. We can do the same again. We can rescue the economy, get people back to work, and set out on the path to being a fairer country. It won't be easy, but it can be done. I also believe that it can happen through politics. That is not to say that politics doesn't need to be reformed: it does. But we have to have some faith in the democratic system, messy and all as it is, because frankly, there is no alternative.

That change must include a determination not to let another crisis like the current one happen again. It is time to bury the politics of the Galway tent, and reform the way we manage our affairs. We have to learn the lessons of the past, and break the link between money and politics, reform the private and public sectors, and stop lurching from one crisis to the next.

The Labour Party played a crucial role in the period when Ireland gained its independence. The struggle we face now is to retain our independence, and our freedom, in economic terms. That's a fight worth winning. We must keep control of our own destiny.

I believe that Ireland is its people. James Connolly once wrote that 'Ireland, without her people, means nothing to me'. Seán O'Casey makes the same point in his plays. We should never forget that the decisions governments make ultimately have an impact on people. People who live and work, and try to get on, in the real world, not just in the world of charts and diagrams. People are not widgets. Our response to the economic crisis has to start from that premise. That it is the people who have lost their jobs, the people who are trying to work hard, play by the rules and care for others who should be at the centre of government's thinking – not just institutions and powerful interests.

I believe that education is the great liberator. I was blessed in having had great teachers, starting with my mother and grandmother, and including people I have met along the way, like Triona Dooney. In the difficult days ahead, we have to protect education, because it is the key to our future. Whoever caused this mess, it wasn't our children.

I believe there is more to life than money. Don't get me wrong: money matters a lot. You have to put the bread on the table. But life is also about 'the rose in the vase'. We have to value and nurture our culture, and cherish our past. And more than that, we have to think about what our children will regard as the yardstick of success. Prosperity matters, but we have to get past measuring people based on what brand of jeans they wear, or what type of car they drive. I hope we will learn from the crisis, and that people will come to measure each other not on what they take out, but on what they put back in. People like Matt Byrne and Joan Miley understood that instinctively.

During the boom years, we sometimes forgot how much we depend on each other. We need to put far greater value and emphasis on service to each other – however great or small. Service is important, and making a contribution to Ireland is an important part of what it means to be Irish.

Finally, no matter how difficult things get – and as I write this, things are certainly very difficult – I believe that we have a duty to hope. We have to keep our eye on the future, to remember that every crisis will ultimately pass, and that we can, if we work together, build a better Ireland.

Index